SHATTERED SELVES

SHATTERED SELVES

Multiple Personality in a Postmodern World

JAMES M. GLASS

CORNELL UNIVERSITY PRESS

Ithaca and London

First published 1993 by Cornell University Press.
Second printing 1994.
First printing, Cornell Paperbacks, 1995.

International Standard Book Number 0-8014-2809-2 (cloth)
International Standard Book Number 0-8014-8256-9 (paper)
Library of Congress Catalog Card Number 92-33928

Printed in the United States of America

*Librarians: Library of Congress cataloging information
appears on the last page of the book.*

⊗ The paper in this book meets the minimum requirements
of the American National Standard for Information Sciences—
Permanence of Paper for Printed Library Materials, ANSI Z39.48-1984.

FOR

Justin, Jeremy, and Jason

Who degrades or defiles the living human body is cursed.

—Walt Whitman, "I Sing the Body Electric"

It is almost amorning. The sun is coming up I sneek [sic] to the door and peek out. Dad is asleep on the steps. Thank you God for letting me sleep some. Do all dads do this to their children? I promise to be good today. You saved me.

Now I lay me down to sleep. I pray the Lord my soul to keep. Please let me die before I wake I pray the Lord my soul to take.

I will say the prayer but I am not a child. I am ten years old. I am not afraid now. Elizabeth.

—From the poetry of a 10-year-old alter personality in a patient diagnosed with multiple personality disorder

CONTENTS

PREFACE

These days the philosophy of postmodernism is argued about in many forums—from academic circles to cinema. It attacks several modernist assumptions regarding rationality, production, domination, and meaning, and in deconstructing these concepts as a tyranny of power often advocates a nihilistic world that will liberate the social order. My concern in this book, however, is with its theory of the self, which often finds the self reduced to a socially constructed self, a self constituted by the intersections of ideology, social practices, and power. Robert Stam's description is typical: "A self is constituted by acquiring the ambient languages and discourses of its world. The self, in this sense, is a kind of hybrid sum of institutional and discursive practices bearing on family, class, gender, race, generation and locale. Ideological development is generated by an intense and open struggle within us for hegemony among the various available verbal and ideological points of view, directions and values" (1988: 120). Most postmodernists reject psychoanalytic views of the self as well as psychiatric intervention.

The philosopher Michel Foucault lays the intellectual groundwork for many of the postmodernist views on what the self is. The Foucaultian position denies the self any internal "being"—there is no inner and outer self, merely practices and ideologies that constitute the self as a consciousness in language. Or, in C. Fred Alford's terms: "Even the real self is an abstraction [in post modernist deconstructionist philosophy], the 'person as rhetorical category,' as Amelie Rorty puts it" (1991: 12).

My approach to the self is very different, and because I see the postmodernist view, if it is not merely a metaphor, as a dangerous advocacy, I evaluate the psychological implications arising from the postmodernist critique of identity, reality, subjectivity, and value. The view I hold derives from a psychoanalytic reading of psychological experience. It is heavily indebted to Melanie Klein and D. W. Winnicott and to the psychoanalytic object-relations tradition generally (a tradition far more sympathetic to maternal presence in forging a strong sense of self-coherence that the psychoanalysis of Jacques Lacan). I take quite seriously the psychoanalytic notion that the constitution of the self involves a complex dialectic between inner realities, including fantasies, hallucinations, and delusions, both conscious and unconscious, and "external," or what Harry Stack Sullivan (1952) called "consensual" reality. But as I shall argue, the most powerful evidence against the postmodernist concept of self comes not from theory but from the words and lives of individuals actually experiencing the terrible psychological dislocation of "multiplicity," women with the psychiatric diagnosis of multiple personality disorder whom I talked with at the Sheppard and Enoch Pratt Hospital in Towson, Maryland. These patients implicitly comment on real problems in a philosophical and cultural position for which nihilism appears to be the guiding philosophical dynamic. (The narratives of men do not appear here because there is little research on male multiple personalities, primarily because so many abused males end up in prisons or jails, where psychiatric research is almost impossible.) I also refer to my experience with schizophrenics in clinical settings.

The cutting edge of the postmodernist theory of self lies with the French theoreticians. My discussion focuses on the French for two reasons: First, postmodernism is a serious philosophy, not simply another relativism or pragmatism, and more complicated than Richard Rorty's adaptation of postmodernism to the American context allows. Such philosophers as Jean Baudrillard and Jean-François Lyotard link the "broken-up self" or identity-less self with the existential demands of nihilism. Second, the French psychoanalytic feminists, accepting certain postmodernist assumptions regarding culture, society, and science, add a fascinating new dimension to the consideration of the modernist notions of a unitary subject and the critique of that "unicity" in the name of "multiplicity." These theorists, including Luce Irigaray, Julia Kristeva, Hélène Cixous, and Catherine Clément, construct powerful arguments for thinking about subjectivity in ways that liberate it from modernist paternalism and authority. Their arguments often depart from those of the postmodernists, especially from those concerning the status of the self, the nature and construction of gender and identity, the presence of suffering, and the place of healing. In connection with both the clinical and the political context of this book, I, from time to time, note these differences.

I begin with a discussion of the postmodern problematic, its context, and its theory of self. In Chapter 2 I present a woman who has created not multiple personalities but multiple realities; this clinical material demonstrates the effects of multiplicity on perception and on the psychoanalytic transference relationship. Chapter 3 considers the psychiatric syndrome multiple personality disorder and its origins in persistent and repeated incestual violation, brutal physical abuse, and the construction of alter selves or personalities to protect from the horror. Chapter 4 brings the French psychoanalytic feminists' view of phallocracy into my own discussion of incest as a form of tyrannical and unconstrained power. Chapters 5 and 6 examine empirical instances of multiple personalities and show, in the context of certain postmodernist views, what it means to live with truly multiple selves. Chapter 7 looks at the idea of asylum in relation to more general issues of psychological fragmentation and to the postmodern problematic, especially to the idealization of schizophrenia proposed by Gilles Deleuze and Félix Guattari.

My sources for the clinical material come from my open-ended discussions with patients at Sheppard-Pratt, discussions that ranged from a few months to over two years. This volume is the third (see Glass 1985, 1989) in a project examining the utterances and experiences of mental patients, a project conducted in the context of arguments, contradictions, and problems in political and social theory. It is my belief that the language of persons suffering severe psychological disconnection and internal fragmentation contains significant commentary on the structure of social and cultural values and assumptions governing political and social practice.

At Sheppard-Pratt, a nonprofit private multiservice hospital, the world of the internal self is unraveled through language, art, dance, and occupational therapy, through constant (critical) scrutiny of therapeutic practice, and through a dedicated effort on the part of the whole staff to be as humane as possible with human beings for whom the world is full of terror, persecution, and often horror. There, where one can observe internal worlds emerge in language and imagery, certain truths about the human condition take on an immanence that unfortunately is hidden from most of society. In spite of the limitations in any kind of institutional context, Sheppard-Pratt provides some relief, or asylum, not only from the terrors of the social world but from the inevitable demons of the internal self which have the power to annihilate being and destroy the possibilities for life.

In the summer of 1976 I became associated with the hospital as a research associate. As a participant observer, I often had—and continue to have—relationships with patients on a one-to-one basis over extended periods of time. I involved myself in the activities of the wards—or halls, as they are called at Sheppard-Pratt. I attended case conferences, lectures, nursing meetings, and clinical review meetings. I familiarized myself as much as possible with the ongoing treatment of patients; my conversations with them occurred on a regular basis at a specific time. I told them I was a political theorist undertaking a research project involving the relationship between philosophical and political issues and psychiatric disturbances. I explained my background, what I hoped to achieve by speaking with them, and why what they had to say might be important. The patients were free to choose whether they wished to participate in my project; they were also free to withdraw at any time. My access was limited only by the consent of the patient and the treating therapist. What I heard in my conversations I shared with the patients' therapists; the patients knew that I maintained an ongoing contact with all aspects of treatment: psychotherapy, dance, art, occupational therapies. Although patients often found it odd that a political theorist would be interested in them, they were cooperative in sharing thoughts and feelings.

I found that it was impossible not to be drawn into these life-worlds, not to be affected, profoundly, by what I heard and saw. Theirs was a universe of immense suffering, alienation, and distortion. Yet when I reviewed the notes and records of my conversations, I discovered metaphors or signs commenting on broader political, social, and cultural issues. What was, however, most remarkable about the dialogues lay in their effect in pushing me both inside and outside of "myself", in generating reflections on self, stirring up unconscious dynamics, and revealing aspects of the self which exist not only in "human nature" but as a form of politics, a debasement and horror that appear in collective forms of organization. To listen to these stories, to witness these patients' narratives, to have access to their histories, pain, and, in some instances, trust, was to experience a world of "research" that was hardly impartial or "objective," in the sense of administering questionnaires and conducting sporadic interviews. Rather, I found myself immersed in an overwhelming subjectivity, in tragic recollections, and in imagery that revealed human lives shattered by the brutality of power, the indifference of society, and the torture arising from the unrestrained and unconscionable desire of others.

The heart of this book lies in the clinical narratives of women suffering from multiple personality disorder. I shall have a great deal to say about this clinical condition, but I stress at the outset that the construction of a space of horror in the self was brought on by continual physical and sexual abuse. When Molly tells how her father forced her to watch chickens being slaughtered, when he insisted she disembowel them, then raped her repeatedly in the shed behind the chicken coop, she speaks of experiences that created a series of identities, each circumscribed in experience and having a specific age, and each provoked by specific horrendous events. Molly's many identities derive from a brutality, exercised by paternal will and power, which had literally no regard for her body or her being.

Kimberly's alter personalities Nea, Tink, Jenny-Precious are produced as a response to the physical torture and abuse that accompanied participation in satanic cult rites, and the accompanying rape by her father, the cult's high priest, week after week. "My life is different," she observes:

> I am not like other people; I live in a world where nothing is certain, not even who I am. Kimberly, me, may disappear for weeks on end; and in her place, there may be this little five-year-old, who desperately struggles with flashbacks to what happened during cult rituals; or I'm a seventeen-year-old angry, sarcastic teenager, who first appeared after being raped by a gang of boys. . . . I am never certain who I will be or when I will be any one of the alters who make up what and who I am. But I know my father did this to me; he took me to the cult meetings; he forced me to do horrible things; I had to watch viciousness done to children and babies. I can't forgive him for that; I won't forgive him; I hate him! I hate what he did to my life. I don't know who to trust or whether I'll ever be able to trust anyone again.

In the survivor of cult abuse, the cult reproduces, at a group level, the horror of the father's violation and the absolute irrevocability of the psychological effects of this degrading power. Not all victims of multiple personality are abused by cults, but a significant number are.

A theme that appears consistently in the narratives of multiple personality disorder is the place of power in the brutalization of the self and in the provocation of a psychological phenomenon that splits identity among a number of unique alter personalities. In none of the accounts offered here did I see that the phenomenon of multiplicity of identity was a creative or playful or regenerative experience. It is not an aesthetic; it is not self-awareness without the constraints or limits of historical knowledge or conventional moralities. It is not symbolically enriching. Multiplicity of identity becomes for these women an ongoing torment, a horror that because of the incessant pain and confusion of living with this condition totally incapacitates them.

Leila was admitted to Sheppard-Pratt after she tried to kill her husband; she had no recollection of what she had done, of driving through her neighborhood streets trying to run him down at four in the morning, because other personalities or identities had been "out." Molly often found burns or cuts on her arms in the morning and had no idea how they got there. During one of our conversations she peeled a soda can as if she were skinning an apple; her fingers started to bleed, but the "out" personality refused to put down the can until she finished her story. Molly's father had frequently threatened to cut her fingers off, to make then bleed, if she ever told. "Daddy . . . he . . . break my fingers . . . hurt, hurt so much . . . I . . . be quiet . . . he said . . . keep your lips shut," a five-year-old alter personality, paralyzed by fear, whispered to me in barely audible tones.

Nora was so terrified by her flashbacks to cult violence ("abreaction") that on the eve of a satanic holiday she would try to kill herself if she were not physically restrained by staff. One morning she had huge bruises on her face and wrists, her eyes were swollen shut, and her body was a grotesque tapestry of black-and-blue splotches. She could barely talk, but she told me that her flashback the previous evening had taken her back to a scene of cult violence. She became so terrified by this impending reliving that to escape its horror she threw herself onto a marble fireplace, banging her head, arms, body as hard as she could. "It didn't work," she said. "Not only could I not kill myself, but I couldn't manage to knock myself out. I wanted to die, though; death was preferable to being back in that time. If staff hadn't stopped me, I might have done it; I might have cracked my skull open."

These stories of physical abuse and indifference to suffering portray the grimmest aspects of human desire: fathers renting their daughters to other men to satisfy gambling debts, using their daughters as private preserves for the exercise of sadistic power, enlisting their children in the violence of cult practices, threatening them with reprisals if they revealed what happened during the satanic rituals; mothers refusing to believe their daughters' stories or sitting silently, blindly, while Daddy raped his litle girl in the next room.

The two years during which I listened to these stories were among the most difficult periods I encountered in over sixteen years of research into mental disorders at Sheppard-Pratt. I was simply not prepared for the reality of what I heard. These women were not "insane" or "crazy" or "demented." Each personality was firmly in touch with "reality," but the personalities themselves were not created as the end result of a course of psychological development, a dialectic. Rather, each grew from singular experiences of abuse; the birth of identity, of multiplicity, derived from another's sickness of desire transmuted into unrestrained power. The "host" personality, the biologically named self, suffered frequent blackouts and finally, when under treatment, usually in the hospital, came to understand that these blackouts meant that other personalities were "out," acting in ways the host personality (when she discovered what had been done) found horrifying and unbelievable. Seeing Molly become increasingly aware of the multiplicity inside her "house of alters," as she called it, was to witness an extraordinary suffering, a despair over ever finding a coherent sense of who she might be or what her potentiality or possibilities could be.

Leila wakes at night and hears people screaming epithets and names at her, but what she hears are the voices inside her own head—not delusions, but alter personalities, specific identities, arguing with each other, screaming, imploring, pleading. For years, Leila lived without the knowledge that these voices or the experiences during her blackouts were those of alter personalities, and Leila found many of them terrifying. One of Leila's alters had planned, in detail, her suicide; she settled on a desolate spot in southeastern Virginia and made plans to end her life by cutting her arteries and bleeding to death in the middle of an empty dirt field. Fortunately the project was never carried out.

Molly experienced different orders of alters. Some were visible, recognizable with names; others were like "trees that move in the fog," vague presences that might from time to time "come in" and make themselves known. But this condition is not insanity, and people with multiple personalities are not psychotic. The brutality of power, the depravity of the force exercised against these women, *is* insanity; the father's power, his indifference to the consequences of physical and psychological violation, is the real madness.

Postmodern philosophers such as Baudrillard and Lyotard use the experience of texts to ground their theories of multiplicity; from these texts they create an aesthetic that celebrates a certain limitlessness and contempt for conventional value, a release from prevailing norms and an embracing of what Lyotard refers to as the "loss of meaning," a "nostalgia for the unattainable," and "a war on totality" (1989: 26,81,82). But for a real person the psychological reality of being multiple, of actually living it out, is an entirely different issue. Or as Richard Shusterman puts it: "Freud implicitly realized what a pricelessly important and yet perhaps fragile achievement the unity of self was, and how difficult and painful such a unified self or self-narration was to construct, and yet how necessary it was to lead any pleasurable version of a good or satisfying life in human society" (1988: 350). When multiplicity appears in reality, as identities frozen in time and trait, when consciousness lives in a psychological nexus distinguished by separable identities each of which possesses idiosyncratic imperatives and languages, the self encounters multiplicity not as an expansive dynamic but as a dreadful commentary on the ends of power, the realization that to live, as Molly puts it, means "enduring a clamor in my head that won't stop, not even in sleep."

It is my belief that these women and their narratives may offer some insight not only into the perversion of power, so eloquently spoken about by the French psychoanalytic feminists, but also into the existential demands of multiple selfhood that lie at the center of much postmodern philosophy.

I thank the patients and staff of the Sheppard and Enoch Pratt Hospital in Towson, Maryland, for their cooperation and participation in this project. Many contributed to my understanding of multiple personality disorder, including Drs. Meyer Liebman, Richard Lowenstein, Laurie Orgel, Miles Quaytman, and Jerry Whitmarsh. Drs. Maria Klement and Clarence Schulz, as they have throughout my research at Sheppard-Pratt, gave of their experience and patience in helping me work through the clinical analysis of special problems associated with the treatment of multiple personality disorder. I am particularly grateful to Dr. Roger Lewin, whose clinical insight and philosophical mind enriched my thinking over the course of this project. Many on the nursing staff shared their time and knowledge: Rosalie Alsop, Jane Goldsborough, and Robert Hurvich, to name just a few.

Bonnie Oppenheimer provided valuable perspectives on the material dealing with satanic cults and cult survivors.

Jean Elshtain, Martha Evans, Jane Flax, Fred Frohock, Sy Ruben-feld and Michael Weinstein gave important critical feedback on the material on postmodernism, psychoanalytic feminism, and multiplicity. I am also indebted to Fred Alford, who read the entire manuscript, Fred Dallmayr, and Victor Wolfenstein, all of whom consistently provided critical direction and encouragement in the development of connections between postmodernism, multiple personality disorder, and political context.

I thank the students in my postmodernism and psychoanalytic feminism seminars, whose lively discussion and curiosity sharpened my theoretical focus.

I am grateful to my typist, Flora Paoli, whose careful reading of the manuscript and its ideas always brought my text to a level of physical clarity which only a skilled, intelligent craftsperson can create.

To my wife, Cyndi, and my children, for their care, support, sensitivity, and welcomed interruptions throughout this project, I owe an enormous debt. Their liveliness and concern sustained me through difficult moments in working with these narratives.

And finally, to the women with multiple personalities, who allowed me to explore their identities, who shared with me frightening histories and images, I come away from this project with a great respect for their courage, strength, and tenacity, for surviving experiences of such horror that their very presence in this world is testimonial to the will to live and to the stubborn refusal to be destroyed by power and injustice.

JAMES M. GLASS

College Park, Maryland

SHATTERED SELVES

1 POSTMODERNISM AND THE MULTIPLICITY OF SELF

What does it mean to speak of multiple (and fragmented) selves? And if the available evidence of multiplicity of self is in women with multiple personalities and with fragmented selves in psychosis, how does this empirical, clinical evidence affect the postmodernists' attack on the unitary self, their views on identity, multiplicity, unicity, fluidity, the power of culture over the self, the function of discourse in defining identity and self, the origin of sexed identity, the experience of fragmentation, the break-up of "rational" structure? (Feldstein and Roof 1989; Flax 1990; Fraser 1989; Lacan 1982; Weedon 1987).

Postmodernism is a philosophy that has reacted strongly against several assumptions of modernity: those concerning progress, history, causality, system, absolutes, meaning, the unitary self, technological judgment, and conformity. It celebrates difference, change, transformation, and flux. Liberation of mind and perception, it argues, requires a liberation of self: to live fully aware of the contingent nature of human value and social facts is to live as a postmodernist. Friedrich Nietzsche is widely regarded as the first postmodernist. The French psychoanalytic feminists are also postmodernists in this respect.[1]

---

[1]Alice Jardine argues that at the "forefront" of postmodernism "is the battle against those systems of mediation which have (over)determined our history: Money, the Phallus

The philosophy criticizes political systems such as "liberalism," "marxism," "communism"—what Lyotard calls the "metanarratives" of history.[2] For him, these metanarratives exercise a debilitating influence on action and perception; they confine thought and impose meaning; therefore, the function of the metanarrative is to assure obedience, acquiescence to systems of value and power which dominate and alienate consciousness. Metanarratives "guarantee . . . legitimacy; as metasubjects, these 'narratives' create the rules of discourse . . . discourse of law . . . the state . . . learning" (1989: 35). Yet, in a postmodern time in which knowledge is "unbalanced" and "speculative unity broken," the metanarrative, or metasubject, constructs false assurances; it mystifies unity and therefore requires a strenuous delegitimation. Lyotard is quite explicit on this point: "The grand narrative has lost its credibility, regardless of what mode of unification it uses, regardless of whether it is a speculative narrative or a narrative of emancipation. . . . the principle of uni-totality—or synthesis under the authority of a metadiscourse of knowledge—is inapplicable" (37, 40). Nancy Fraser and Linda J. Nicholson write that Lyotard "infers the illegitimacy of large historical stories, normative theories of justice, and social-theoretical accounts of macrostructures which institutionalize inequity" (1990: 24).

This aspect of Lyotard's social theory—the critique of metanarratives—is one that the French psychoanalytic feminists take quite seriously, particularly in regard to the delegitimation of phallocentric values and assumptions. Further, Lyotard's questioning of scientific legitimation and "proof" finds a theoretical affinity in the feminists' effort to break up constituted realities, to reflect on what Luce Irigaray calls the "fluidity" of feminine experience, its unpredictable multiplicity and variability, and, with Julia Kristeva, to treat and

---

and the Concept as Privileged operators of meaning. To that extent feminism is certainly *intrinsic*" to postmodernism (1985: 101). Both are involved in similar projects: a rejection of "Anthropomorphism, Humanism and Truth. . . . It is in France . . . that, in my opinion, this rethinking has taken its strongest conceptual leaps, as 'philosophy,' 'history,' and 'literature' have attempted to account for the crisis-in-narrative that is modernity" (25). Yet there are significant differences, particularly in terms of feminist criticisms of self, representation, and meaning. "Why do these two modes of inquiry, feminism and postmodernism, prove so resistant to each other at these intersections when their projects are so irresistibly linked?" (61).

[2]For an insightful discussion of Lyotard's "rhetoric of heterogeneity, incommensurability, language-games, and difference" (223), see Morris 1988.

heal patients without resorting to fixed, immobile conceptions of cure, identity, and normality. Each would agree with Lyotard's observation (also an argument at the heart of Richard Rorty's postmodernism): "Science plays its own game; it is incapable of legitimating the other language games . . . it is incapable of legitimating itself, as speculation assumed it could" (1989: 40). Lyotard's postmodernism affirms individuality, in the sense of the ahistoricity of the self, and rejects the enslavement of self to absolutes that are themselves products of history and time. He is skeptical about the role of institutional "politics" and the possibility of "political" solutions; in addition, he ignores the concept of agency in promoting and sustaining political change.

Seyla Benhabib takes issue with Lyotard; she believes his philosophy, his "justice of multiplicities," may lead to a "new conservatism or a relativism," that his "heterogeneity of difference" can be dangerous politically (1990: 115–16). Benhabib speaks of a "polytheism of values" that may provoke a real cynicism over the ends of political life. "The line between truth and deception, consensus and coercion disappear in Lyotard's agnostics" (116). Further, she says, Lyotard's insistence on the "incommensurability of language games, in the name of polytheism, may generate moral and political indifference; the call for innovation, experimentation, and play may be completely dissociated from social reform and institutional practice, and the activation of differences may not amount to a democratic respect of the right of the other to be, but to a conservative plea to place the other, because of her otherness, outside the pale of our common humanity and mutual responsibility" (122).

For such theorists as Irigaray, Cixous, and Clément, however, "heterogeneity" may lead to a politics of difference; rather than being nihilist or relativistic, their political positions could be fairly described as "plural" and decentered or decentralized.

The cultural critique of postmodernism attacks consumerism, technological modernity (what Baudrillard calls the "hyperreal"), and the values and orientations of bureaucracy and bureaucratic rationality. It raises serious and important questions about the nature of interpretation and value in a world defined by possessive individualism, domination, and power.

Richard Rorty sees the postmodern deconstruction of science, rationality, objectivity and "truth" as adding a refreshing skepticism to intellectual inquiry: "We are making the purely *negative* point that we would be better off without the traditional distinctions between knowledge and opinion, construed as the distinction between truth as correspondence to reality and truth as a commendatory term for well justified belief. . . . we pragmatists do not have a theory of truth, much less a relativistic one" (1989: 11).

Further, postmodernists have added a significant critique to psychoanalytic feminism (Conley 1984; Flax 1987, 1990; Miller 1986; Sprengnether 1990), particularly in their analyses of domination and patriarchy, what Luce Irigaray (1985a) calls the phallocentric culture; Jane Gallop, "Lacanian Conceit" (1982a: 15); Catherine Clément, "women's causality" (Cixous and Clément 1986: 6); and Hélène Cixous, "Write yourself: your body must make itself heard" (1986: 97). It is a philosophy that reveals frightening contradictions in the social, cultural, and political assumptions of modern society.

The Postmodernist Self

The problematic I am concerned with, however, is one of postmodernism's central psychological and political arguments: the praising and celebration of the multiplicity of self. In the postmodernist view, theories of self derive from the social and cultural practices specific to a historic epoch and currents of power whose interest it is to define the self in ideological terms (Foucault 1979). One cannot, in this view, speak of an "unconscious" or an "unconscious fantasy" or repression or splitting or projection, and so on, because the very existence of these psychoanalytic concepts depends on psycho-historical perspectives that involve the use of an interpretive power. All social practices, particularly those that focus on mental illness or psychotherapy, possess power in the culture. It is that power, according to a point of view largely elaborated by Michel Foucault, which defines what the self is and what "meanings" are to be found in the self. The self, its identity, is filled out through the defining effects of "epistemes," conjunctions of knowledge and power embodied in social interests.

In their insistence on freeing the self from any historical or structural conception of what the self is, the postmodernists reject, in coming to an understanding of what identity "is," the influence of infancy, the psychoanalytic notion of the preoedipal, the Freudian concept of the unconscious (drive theory), and the idea that actions of the self may be represented in severe forms of internal psychological conflict whose origins lie in primitive emotional symbolization.

Much of the postmodernist critique sees the essentialist self as static, immovable, and therefore representing fixed, immutable modernist assumptions. It views the "Freudian" self as the self of bourgeois early-twentieth century Vienna and therefore not responsive to modern concerns. The modern psychoanalytic object-relations self, the postmodernists argue, is the self of interpersonal theories of human identity defined by society and therefore derivative and ideological. Feminist critics such as Irigaray (1985a) and Cixous (1986, 1990) see the essentialist self as embodying patriarchal conceptions of static hardness: impermeable, oppressive structures that suggest the worst of paternal domination.

Postmodernist and poststructuralist theorists reject any notion of a self which implies that deeper structures may be necessary for the self's orientation and capacity in the world. To posit the distinction between healthy and not-healthy, the argument goes, is to find oneself lost in a labeling morass that simply reflects the differing social practices buttressed by power. What matters for the postmodernist is how the self experiences life in all its contingency; life becomes a work of art, or life is lived as an aesthetic (Wilde 1981).[3] To attain

---

[3]The aesthetic and its presence in language takes on a kind of power that postmodernism is ostensibly attacking. Huyssen writes, "The insight that the subject is constituted in language and the notion that there is nothing outside the text have led to the privileging of the aesthetic and the linguistic which aestheticism has always promoted to justify its imperial claims. The list of 'no longer possibles' (realism, representation, subjectivity, history, etc., etc.) is as long in post-structuralism as it used to be in modernism, and it is very similar indeed" (1990: 259). He argues that this insistence on "no longer possibles" depletes the theory and creates a kind of conceptual atrophy. "One may well ask whether the theoretically sustained self-limitation to language and texuality has not been too high a price to pay; and whether it is not this self-limitation (with all it entails) which makes this post-structuralist modernism look like the atrophy of an earlier aestheticism rather than its innovative transformation" (261).

that artistry or what Henry Kariel (1989) calls "play" or "playfulness" requires the self be fluid, unconstrained, or, in other words, "multiple" or fragmented.

A notable exception to the antipathy to psychoanalytic theory lies in the writings of the French psychoanalytically oriented feminists, although they share many of the epistemological assumptions of the postmodernists. Though somewhat eclectic in their use of psychoanalytic models (this is particularly true of Kristeva), they often speak of identity, its origins and its effects on the self, in ways that show the influence of psychoanalytic theorizing. Symbols, mythic imagery, storytelling, recollections from childhood, reflections on paternal power, maternal presence, appear with some frequency in the work of Kristeva, Irigaray, and Cixous. Their writings treat multiplicity much more sensitively than do other postmodernists; they give the concept more context in issues pertaining to gender, suffering, and the impact of phallocratic or paternal power on the feminine body and psyche. Andreas Huyssen, however, contributes an important insight the French feminists often ignore: "Doesn't poststructuralism, where it simply denies the subject altogether, jettison the chance of challenging the *ideology of the subject* (as male, white and middle-class) by developing alternative and different notions of subjectivity?" (1990: 264).

Although I recognize that postmodernism as a social theory involves more than its critique of the unitary subject, I want to emphasize that the psychological dimension of its theory, the concept of self, rests heavily on the desirability of multiplicity of selves. It is one thing to speak of multiple moods and interests or an infinite variety of ethical and moral choices. It is an entirely different matter to live as if the universe, the world, existence were fragments, without connection. Some linear connection to one's own history and to the existent world is necessary even to organize the simplest of tasks. Yet the clinical naïveté of postmodern theorists in this respect is often quite astounding. For example, Sandra Harding writes: "I argue for the primacy of fragmented identities but only for those healthy ones constructed on a solid and non-defensive core identity, and only within a unified opposition, a solidarity against the culturally dominant forces of unitarianism" (1986: 247). Harding's approach has been criticized as theoretically contradictory. Christine Di Stefano accuses it of slipping in modernist assumptions in a generally "postmodern" analysis: "Harding has smuggled a forbidden vocabulary into her analysis, a vocabulary whose connotative context lies in the very modernist, humanist, rationalist discourse she is presumably repudiating. Criteria such as these, of "health," "solidity," "nondefensiveness," "identity," and "unity" partake of the very ontology disallowed by postmodernism; they all require standards of normalcy, of judgment, of hierarchical distinctions which must be rooted within some organizing and legitimating ground or framework" (1990: 76–77). But Harding can't have it both ways: in a clinical sense, if an identity is fragmented, it lacks a coherent or cohesive frame within a given time and place. Fragmented identities are disoriented, confused, often schizoid or schizophrenic.

But that is precisely the problem. I come back to this time and again: if the postmodernist theory of multiplicity is to mean more than an emotional pluralism, which would give that theory a liberal/ pragmatic cast, it must refer to fragmentation as a function of identity. If that is the case, how does one live with a fragmented identity? That very practical question never seems to surface in these theoretical discussions.

In this respect, Di Stefano raises an important point about the implications of multiplicity: "If we are encouraged to embrace fractured identities, we are inevitably drawn to the forbidden question: Fractured with respect of *what*?" (1990: 76). This "what" becomes the source of a new theory of identity or subjectivity, thereby revealing circularity in the postmodern wish to have what amounts to an "organized" fragmentation. Di Stefano asks, "Can fractured identities be embraced without the parallel construction of new fictions of counter-identity?" (76). Probably not, so that the postmodern argument is not only abstract but psychologically thin or naive. If a counteridentity is posed, then the analysis comes back to its starting point: the issue of a unified self or a theory of subjectivity.

From a clinical point of view, a fractured identity lacks a center, a cohesiveness that might provide for the self an orientation or stability in a world that in its political, cultural, and social manifestations is chaotic enough. Although multiple personalities do in fact function in the world, the nature of that functioning is dramatically transformed when consciousness comes to an awareness of its multiplicity, the alter personalities literally living within the self.

If multiple personality disorder and schizophrenia are extreme forms of what the postmodernists idealize (for example, Deleuze and Guattari's idealization of the schizophrenic as a "revolutionary"), then there is something terribly wrong in the postmodernist interpretation of what multiplicity or fragmentation of self means, and questions of meaning become quite appropriate when one addresses the practicalities involved in living with broken-up identities. The writing of the French feminists is not nearly as disconnected or detached from the pragmatics of multiplicity as are the writings of poststructuralist philosophers and literary critics. But although they place more emphasis on gender and the construction of a feminine *gestalt* as forms of agency or change—Cixous and Irigaray frequently allude poetically to the construction of feminine identity—they too are at times sketchy in thinking through what the practical effects of multiplicity are and what they mean.

The Body of Text, the Place of Suffering

It is all well and good, this process of what Rorty calls "breaking down . . . oppositions . . . the new fuzziness" (21, 20), the critique of objectivity, moral truth, and reason (Lyotard's "rhetoric of heterogeneity" [Morris 1988]). But the questioning of science, Rorty's muted postmodern pragmatism, and what Hilary Lawson describes as "the view that meaning is undecidable and therefore truth unattainable" (1989: xii) should not be taken as indicative of the theory's cutting edge regarding self and identity. If philosophy has anything to do with life and experience, if it influences those who read it (are not philosophers teachers?), then the celebration of multiplicity of self ought to be separated from more general postmodern critiques of patriarchy, technological society, instrumental rationality, and scientific objectivity.

I am not unsympathetic to many of the postmodernist arguments, and I can respond to Robert Stam's statement that postmodernism encourages a plurality of discourses, "a fundamentally non-unitary, constantly shifting cultural field in which the most varied discourses exist in shifting multi-valanced oppositional relationships" (1988: 33). Stam's perspective is similar to what Kristeva speaks of when she finds in Philippe Soller's novel *H* "music that is inscribed in language, becoming the object of its own reasoning, ceaselessly, and until saturated, overflowing, and dazzling sense has been exhausted. . . . It whisks you from your comfortable position; it breathes a gust of dizziness into you, but lucidity returns at once, along with music" (1980: 7). This praise of a liberating, non-linear form of human presence is echoed by Cixous: "I must become a fabulous opera and not the area of the known. Understand it the way it is: always more than one, diverse, capable of being all those it will at one time be, a group acting together, a collection of singular beings that produce the enunciation. Being several and insubordinable, the subject can resist subjugation" (1974: 307).

Where do these metaphors lead us? To be "fabulous opera" requires a sense of self which keeps the strains, the melodic lines, the counterpoint, the text, in order; opera *is* mammoth organization. It cannot sustain melodic or lyrical chaos. And to be "more than one" involves a sense of what one is as a sentient being attached to identifiable pasts and histories. Awareness of a script presupposes some sense or knowledge of structure. Too often, however, postmodern theory is cavalier about the historical self—precisely that aspect of the self which enables it to organize, metabolize, and internalize the plurality of "becoming." Without that capacity, the self finds itself, as in schizophrenia or multiple personality disorder, overwhelmed by its various manifestations, its multiplicity. Cixous, at least, as opposed to the Foucaultian poststructuralists, is sensitive to the human and emotional consequences of this "fabulous opera," to the effects fragmentation has on bodies and psyche, to the importance of what Domna C. Stanton calls the "maternal metaphor" (1986: 163).[4]

[4]Stanton speaks about the preoedipal self as an object of "focus" for Cixous, as well as for Kristeva and Irigaray. Language serves the effort of recovering the "prehistory of women . . . abducted and buried alive by man, like Persephone, that [feminine] past can be recaptured as a 'rebeginning' insists Cixous, through the de-repression of unconscious or archaic memories" (1986: 185). She quotes from Cixous's *Illa*: "The voice is the uterus . . .

Cixous's play *Portrait of Dora* reveals this empathy in relation to hysteria. In her fascinating and provocative discussion of this play, Martha Noel Evans draws out Cixous's concept of multiplicity and the fluidity of identity. "For all the characters in the play, the answer to the question, 'Who is in whose place?' is multiple, indefinite. . . . The doors of Dora's desire flutter not in a discursive linear chronology but in a rhythmic pulsation or flux, always in process of being both opened and closed. For her, opposites are not negations of one another, but part of a continuous movement of double linking: 'Me in myself . . . In you'" (1987: 173, 180). Evans's analysis of *Portrait of Dora* provides a crucial insight into how multiplicity, as a phenomenology of experience, governs human behavior and action. Cixous uses multiplicity not so much to celebrate fragmentation as to speak about the complex process of human interaction and transformation, especially in relation to what we project into others. It is almost as if in *Portrait of Dora* she is constructing the literary equivalent of what psychoanalysis calls projective identification.

William Corlett argues that the concept of abandon needs to be taken seriously when one thinks about postmodernism: "Names like Foucault and Derrida can . . . be drawn closer to political discourse by using *abandon* in the sense of losing self-control or giving in to the accidental, chaotic aspect of any structure" (1989: 3). Yet, if one takes the concept of abandon (and I would also add *abandonment*) seriously in looking at the concept of self, some important questions arise. Multiple personalities and schizophrenics are the abandoned selves of our time; and if abandon has any paradigmatic psychological property, it is to be found in these dislocated and disconnected lives. Jacques Derrida's "innocence of becoming" (1978:292) finds itself in such persons transformed into horror; to idealize abandon as a kind of existential model, therefore, seems to be idealizing cruelty and ignoring the functions of empathy in holding the self and community together.

The postmodernist view drives at an appreciation for multiple

---

Voice. Inexhaustible milk . . . The lost mother. Eternity: voice mixed with milk" (1985: 167). The emphasis is on interiority and, as Stanton describes it, "the pleasures of an expansive writing fertile with possibles and the uniquely maternal experience of arrival, issue, and separation" (1986: 168).

forms of experience, what Georges Bataille (1985) calls the "hetero-geneity of excess," what Cixous sees as the imperative of feminine writing.[5] But to handle these kinds of experiences, their diversity or excess, requires an inner resiliency capable of psychologically with-standing the onslaughts of a fragmented existential field. Kristeva and Irigaray, as therapists, deal on a day-to-day basis with the emo-tional impact of these "onslaughts." In *Angst*, Cixous draws this out in extraordinary detail:

> Madness! Madness! what have I done? . . . Thoughts are dan-gerous. It tears me apart to see the body created for you, up to its neck in the jaws of the Monster Amnesia. . . . What do the jaws want? I turn over in bed wallowing in Loss. . . . Oh God! What have I done to you that you want me to soil myself? I am pros-trate, my sheep's gown tucked up. Help, my life is slipping away. . . . Who wants to drive me to despair? If it's not you, it's god. So it's me too. . . . Gradually, I have become more and more deeply, more and more carnally, tangled up in sheets full of vermin—and under my life gown my vile flesh. . . . My crav-ing to complain in the bitterness of my blood and the shit of my body. To describe my scarred skin to God, so he would know me by my vermin. Make a statement of my wounds, so that he could check my accounts. . . . I had been festering for so long. (1985: 76–78)

Roland Barthes describes the "text of bliss . . . the text that im-poses a state of loss . . .that unsettles the reader's historical, cul-tural, psychological assumptions, the consistency of his tastes, values, memory, brings to crisis his relations with language" (1975: 14, 37).[6] To sustain that kind of plurality necessitates a self ready to organize the chaos, to assimilate forces attempting to pull or tear the self apart. But the absence of this self is also part of the problem

---

[5] "Feminine" writing for Cixous should reflect the essential nature of feminine presence; it should change, transform, shift, disrupt, and occasionally turn back on itself. "Cixous coins words and distorts words, plays with words and with syntax, with meanings and suggestions, with metaphors and illusions, alliterations and rhythms. Few French writers since Rabelais have taken the liberties with language she dares to take" (from Sankovitch 1988: 134).

[6] Or in Nancy Miller's terms: "Dispersion and fragmentation, the theft of language and the subversion of the stereotype attract Barthes as critical styles of desire and deconstruc-tion" (1988: 111).

with the postmodernist view. It takes as the ground of experience texts, not bodies (again, with the notable exception of the psychoanalytic feminists); words, not survivors; letters, not feelings. To endure the Barthesian "moment," or *jouissance*, requires not only a firm grounding in reality but a self strong enough to pull out of the chaos.

Barthes continues, "We read [the text] . . . the way a fly buzzes around a room: with sudden, deceptively decisive turns, fervent and futile" (14). It is an entirely different matter for *persons* to live with selves as chaotic as the buzzing of a fly; if this is meant as metaphor for self, it is an extremely demanding and disorienting one. What happens inside a text and what happens inside the self are often radically different forms of being and becoming. What Terry Eagleton says about Berthold Brecht's work, "the dismantling of our given identities through art" (1983: 191) is a much different proposition from the psychological dismantling of identity. The "deconstructing" of identity is what happens in psychosis.

If the postmodernist theory of self is to be understood as more than an aesthetic, if it is to be taken seriously as a philosophy, an argument about living in the world, a concept of self, then "deconstructed" *real* people might provide something of a necessary perspective. Clinically, one doesn't "know . . . internal fragmentation" (Eagleton 1983: 191); one *suffers* it. Cixous's *Angst* is an extraordinary testimonial to this fact. The pleasure of gazing on fragmentation is quite different from the actual experience of living it.

Even the body in postmodernist thought is interpreted as a kind of text, a language; its significance and presence appears through its context in language.[7] Lacan's notion of the subject as being produced socially but controlled through the language of the symbolic is taken literally. For example, Arthur Kroker and David Cook write, "The body is a power grid, tattooed with all the signs of cultural excess on its surface, encoded from within by the language of desire, broken into at will by the ideological interpellation of the subject, and, all the while, held together as a fictive and concrete unity by the illusion of *misrecognition*" (1986: 26).

---

[7]For an interesting discussion of the linguistic roots of poststructuralism and the limitations in its philosophical position (particularly in relation to the French structuralists), see T. G. Pavel (1990).

In her article "Castration or Decapitation," Cixous speaks of a "kind of disengagement, not the detachment that is immediately taken back but a real capacity to lose hold and let go [which] takes the metaphorical form of wandering, excess, risk of the unreckonable" (1981: 53). Yet persons who find themselves psychically unhinged, emotionally "decapitated" not as metaphor but as lived experience, suffer from a disengagement that leads not to knowledge or irony but to pain, victimization, and incapacity. A real letting go, then, in selves lacking a strong center or "subjectivity" (and I will come back to this concept in the next chapter), sets the stage not for irony but for tragedy. It is this tragic dimension that the aesthetic and textual dimension of postmodernism has ignored, although the feminists demonstrate a deep empathy for the tragedy sustained by women through the history of patriarchy and the exercise of phallocentric power.

Fred Pfeil, in an essay mildly critical of the postmodernist position, speaks of "the appeal of (as Deleuze and Guattari might put it . . .) the new, unrestricted schizoid self, awash in its desiring flows, freely floating in the warm, amniotic currents of the Kristevan or Barthesian semiotic, untethered by memory to any fixed sense of the self" (1988: 70–71). In clinical reality such selves are hardly bathed in a "warm, amniotic current"; rather, the existence of schizoid or schizophrenic selves is encumbered by abandonment, isolation, coldness, and death. Pfeil asks, "What does it mean, then, that we have . . . what is by now a veritable legacy of theoretical texts, concepts, and arguments which criticize classical narrative and the unitary bourgeois self in the name of heteroglossia, dissemination, decentering, the flux of the semiotic, and a new, post-oedipal, nonunitary subjectivity which [in Cixous's terms] 'being several and insubordinable . . . can resist subjugation'?" (72).

Is, in fact, the concept of a unitary self restrictive and debilitating? One can live with a healthy postmodern skepticism toward truth, absolutes, causality, and rationality yet at the same time acknowledge and recognize how critical a core sense of self is to the project of life itself. It is therefore necessary to look beyond the ideological criticism of unicity, as instrument of patriarchy and power, toward its psychological significance. From the perspectives of schizophrenics and of women with multiple personalities, the postmodern "ever shifting bricolage and blur" (Pfeil 1988: 73) imply a

radical insensitivity to feelings, specifically the feelings of abandonment, terror, and implosion.

The criticism here is not with the Foucaultian or postmodern
project of deconstructing discourses, *"uncoupl*[ing] and *disrupt*[ing]
the prevailing array of discourses through which subject identities
are formed" (Bennett 1982; quoted in Pfeil 1988: 73). But it is one
thing to engage in a postmodern project as a matter of literary or
philosophic criticism, and an entirely different issue to suggest it as
a psychological proposition underlying the existence of the self and
the political space. What Pfeil calls "the broth of Barthesian *jouissance"* becomes for the woman with multiple personalities or for the
schizophrenic a descent into terror. Real selves that live out the psychological imperatives of multiplicity have nothing in common with
selves deconstructed in texts. Pfeil argues that the poststructuralist
feminist critique of any "stable identity . . . [and] advocacy of a resis-
tent, mercurial subjectivity-in-slippage" may be *"strategically* com-
prehensible" (76) in the sense of a political attack on male-domi-
nated hierarchies. But I want to emphasize that subjectivity-in-
slippage *clinically* denotes selves in terrible distress and pain.

Pfeil, though accepting certain postmodernist perspectives, finds
it essential to connect the uncoupled self to some "new *collective* subjectivities . . . communities capable of purposive action towards
shared ends and goals" (76). Although his argument is laudable, real
disrupted, uncoupled, and slipped-away selves possess little talent
for the organizing tasks necessary to create such communities. The
postmodernists can't have it both ways: ahistorical selves, these
"bricolage identities," who are still capable of complex tasks of organization and control.

The Deconstruction of the Self and
the "Real World"

The postmodern critique of the essentialist or unitary self occurs
in a psychological vacuum. Its critique of modernity, particularly the
feminist critique of paternal power and rationality, should be separated from the proposition that the only way to free culture from the
historical legacy of patriarchy is to advocate the deconstruction of

identity. (This is a side of the problematic which requires even more attention from the psychoanalytic feminists.) The evaluation of theories of power, domination, and patriarchy is important and useful, but to utilize schizophrenia as a model for the "ideal" deconstructed identity (Deleuze and Guattari's argument in *Anti-Oedipus*—which has little in common with that of the psychoanalytic feminists) is irresponsible and insensitive to the human costs of this illness.

An irony of postmodernism is that its central psychological proposition, the break-up of the unitary self, works against its more public or political objectives. Or, to put it another way: the elimination of the patriarchal self of bourgeois liberalism, that self's obsession with domination and its antifeminism, might be attained without the ideological proclamation that identity is dead. Broken selves have no political meaning or value; what meaning they have lies in the language and metaphors of tragedy. The dismantling of the unified subject of modernism is simply insufficient as a response both to the psychological problems accompanying fragmentation and the real political contradictions of late capitalism. As Terry Eagleton puts it: "Nor is the dismantling of the unified subject a revolutionary gesture in itself. Kristeva rightly perceives that bourgeois individualism thrives on such a fetish, but her work tends to halt at the point where the subject has been fractured and thrown into contradiction" (1983: 191).

This theoretical impasse exists in much of psychoanalytic feminism, particularly those aspects of the theory influenced by postmodernism. Even Irigaray's intriguing concept of "fluidity," as a way of thinking about feminine identity, lacks a practical translation of theoretical metaphor into lived reality. How does one make sense out of a "fluid" self? The metaphor may be too diffuse, too lacking a content that orients consciousness toward action and relationship. Yet her chapter on "fluid mechanics" in *This Sex Which Is Not One* paints a picture of feminine consciousness radically at odds with phallocratic "solidity"; the imagery allows the self to traverse the "zone of silence" established by the law of the father and to discover meaning and identity in forms of expression (discourse) which are "by nature, unstable" (112). "Woman," Irigaray observes, "cannot hear herself" (111).

There is a certain fascinating dimension or allusiveness to this

view of the breakdown of the unitary bourgeois subject and the liberation of feminine multiplicity, feminine identity. For example,
Clément writes, "Festival and madness. The feminine figure who
crystallizes around herself the swirling glances of a threatened culture. And not far away—revolutionary myths, the figure of liberty"
(Cixous and Clément 1986: 26). Or Cixous (in ibid.):

> If there is a self proper to woman, paradoxically it is her capac-
> ity to de-propriate herself without self-interest: endless body,
> without "end," without principal "parts"; if she is a whole, it is
> a whole made up of parts that are wholes, not simple, partial
> objects but varied entirety, moving and boundless change, a
> cosmos where eros never stops traveling, vast astral space. She
> doesn't revolve around a sun that is more star than the stars. [87]

> That does not mean that she is undifferentiated magma; it
> means that she doesn't create a monarchy of her body or her
> desire. . . . woman, writing herself, will go back to this body that
> has been worse than confiscated. [87, 97]

> I am spacious singing Flesh: onto which is grafted no one
> knows which I—which masculine or feminine, more or less hu-
> man but above all living, because changing I. [88]

Eagleton goes on: "For Brecht, by contrast, the dismantling of
our given identities through art is inseparable from the practice of
producing a new kind of human subject altogether which would
need to know not only internal fragmentation but social solidarity,
which would experience not only the gratifications of libidinal language but the fulfillments of fighting political injustice" (1983: 191).
His is, of course, a much different, more ideological vision from the
French feminists' approach to human possibility. Eagleton expects
too much: internally fragmented selves, fractured egos, as the van-
guard of new political collectivities. I can imagine no person more
appalled at the prospects of "solidarity" or "collectivity" than the
schizophrenic.

More radical statements about the postmodernist conception of
self and reality come from what are called the "surfictionists"; their
literature scrambles reality and blurs self/other boundaries. Ray-
mond Federman says of the "new novel" or of what Richard McCor-

mick (1991) calls the "new subjectivity" that "it abolishes absolute knowledge and what passes for reality; it even states, defiantly, that reality as such does not exist" (1978: 122; also see Schechner 1982). Federman also proclaims that "the new novel invents its own reality, cuts itself off from referential point with the external world (122). . . . The real world is somewhere else. . . . a world no longer to be known, but to be imagined, to be invented" (124). Or, in Ronald Sukenick's terms: "Reality doesn't exist, time doesn't exist, personality doesn't exist" (1969: 41; also see Federman's "Surfiction—Four Propositions in Form of an Introduction," 1975).

But this is precisely the epistemological fate of psychological fragmentation: "the real world is somewhere else" or the real world is simply what the imagination projects it to be. And to multiple personalities, reality appears in a number of differing forms depending on which alter personality happens to be present to consciousness. Federman writes, "I want to tell a story that cancels itself as it goes"; yet this cancelation is typical of schizophrenia. Delusion persistently destroys what came before; each delusional subset is independent of the previous ones. Sukenick's words in *The Death of the Novel*, could be used as a description of the phenomenology of schizophrenia: "Reality has become a literal chaos. . . . If reality exists, it doesn't do so *a priori*, but only to be put together. . . . The world is real because it is imagined" (47). . . . "I thrive on chaos" (100).

Literature breaks the hold of reality; in Kristeva's words: "Literature reveals a certain knowledge and sometimes the truth itself about an otherwise repressed, nocturnal, secret and unconscious universe. . . . It thus redoubles the social contract by exposing the unsaid, the uncanny. . . . [Literature and its scrambling of reality] makes a game, a space of fantasy and pleasure, out of the abstract and frustrating order of social signs, the words of everyday communication." Yet, she goes on, while literature serves the ends of imagination, the utterances of persons suffering from multiplicity also have the power to reveal the "repressed, nocturnal, secret and unconscious universe" (1986: 207). Literature or art creates its own rules; aesthetic is bound by the limits of imagination (Lederman's "I wallow in chaos"). With survivors and victims, aesthetic finds itself defined by history; and ultimately it is the space of Lacan's real, with all its horror and pain, that the self draws on in its narrative reconstructions. Or, in Cixous's terms: "There are texts that are made of flesh" (1990: 27). In the worlds of psychotic and psychically dissociated texts, as Kristeva has argued in *Black Sun*, the imagination functions as witness, as a reporting and participation, an intimacy fed by history, and ultimately is dependent on whatever brutality, cruelty, and love that history throws in its path.

In literature, the text itself derives from an internal dialogue, a construction riveting time within the bounds of the author's imagination. It is an effort, in language, to publicize truth; again, Cixous's imagery is pertinent: "The scope between the writer and truth, that opening, is probably where the writing slides by" (1990: 9). The writing and its effects on the public may be disruptive: "Writing should dedicate itself to the truth which is violent" (22) or at least to a truth that is not always palatable or pleasant in its unraveling or "telling." For Cixous, the postmodern position takes language as the critical instrument for unmasking the oppressiveness both of self and reality. Or, in Franz Kafka's terms: "Books must be the axe to break the frozen sea within us" (from Kafka's *Correspondence*, 1904; quoted in Cixous 1990: 26).[8]

Kristeva: Subjectivity and Fragmentation

Kristeva, a practicing psychoanalyst, is more sympathetic than are the postmodernists to the notion of a cohesive identity, or at least to its possibility, and she is intensely sensitive to the pain of disintegrated selves. She sees, listens to, and treats individuals whose identities, whose "subjectivities" have been shattered, who live in what she calls "emptiness," whose beings literally lack coherence or meaning. Witnessing this language of pain, she finds herself, as Toril Moi suggests, caught between the more radical deconstructionists of feminism and the psychoanalytic project committed to rescuing or healing the subject.

When speaking of herself, Kristeva argues that "I myself, at the

---

[8]The entirety of this particular quotation is interesting: "What we need are the books which work upon us as a terrible event, as a stroke of happiness which hurts us, as the death of one whom we love more than ourselves would hurt us, as when we were lost in forests without human beings around, as suicide. Books must be the axe to break the frozen sea within us, that's what I believe."

deepest level of my wants and desires, am unsure, centerless and divided" (1987: 8), she refers to her psychoanalytic knowledge gained through discourse: I can be divided, yet I know I am divided; analysis makes me aware of my essential "multiplicity" as a human being, but I am capable of making sense out of that multiplicity. I understand myself as a bounded and gendered presence. I have learned to distance myself from dangers inherent in maternal and paternal power. I exist as a person aware of my own history and its effect on me. Whatever is divided within myself appears as difference in mood, taste, style, action, and value; but my identity, my sense of who I am within a given history and time, remains strong and resilient. I am therefore able to act and be in the world without finding myself overwhelmed by ideology or instrumental power; I also have a firm enough grasp of causality to keep from falling into the amorphous chaos of delusion or the disconnected frames of an internal world detached from any known or recoverable history.

Kristeva's sense of herself as divided does not eliminate her "capacities for commitment and trust but makes them, literally and in no other way, *playable* (in the sense that a piece of music is playable"; 8). Yet Kristeva, as an analyst, knows that to make sense out of one's centerlessness requires a firm sense of a core self: a gendered, bounded self defended from regression or split-off passions, what W. Ronald D. Fairbairn calls "introjected objects in inner reality" (1944: 82). Such knowledge of self comes not only from an exhaustive examination of one's own disguised and often hidden history but from a psychological past that has managed to maintain the interstices between inner and outer reality. Unlike Derrida, Lyotard, and Baudrillard, she would not leave the self without identity: rather than idealize "becoming" and flux (the Heraclitian foundations of deconstructionism), she sees the subject as a presence in the midst of flux, but a subject that would be lost without an orienting faculty, an identity, a subjectivity. Moi summarizes Kristeva's project: "The Kristevan subject is a subject-in-process (*sujet en procès*) but a subject nevertheless. We find her [Kristeva] carrying out once again a difficult balancing act between a position which would deconstruct subjectivity and identity altogether, and one that would try to capture these entities in an essentialist or humanist mould" (1986: 13).

Further, the reality of suffering, fractured egos, torn selves, creates, paradoxically, a certain sympathy for a concept of subjectivity. Again, Moi: "It is Kristeva's psychoanalytic practice that makes her put the case with such force for an unstable and always threatened, yet nevertheless real and necessary, form of subjectivity. The analyst is after all engaged in the task of healing her patients, and has therefore to provide them with some kind of 'identity' which will enable them to live in the world, that is to say, within the symbolic order, dominated by the law" (13–14).

Kristeva, then, in her practice (her *praxis*) is concerned with bodies, not just texts; her interest is not only interpretation but also change—but change that presupposes the recovery of a subject with an identity rooted in a sense of past, present, and future.[9] She desires change, but change that preserves the integrity of the subject. In the first epigraph of her *Psychoanalysis and the Polis* she quotes from Marx and Engels' *Theses on Feuerbach*: "Up until now philosophers have only interpreted the world. The point now is to change it" (1982: 302).

A feminist who describes a woman "trapped within the frontiers of her body and even of her species [who] feels *exiled* . . . by the very powers of generalization intrinsic to language" (1986b: 296), Kristeva sees change, unlike Lacan, not only as analysis of the symbolic, the paternal law, the oedipal situation, but as an effort to ground identity, subjectivity, in a set of relations having to do with the maternal, the feminine. "Self" has concrete human representations and masks for any practicing psychoanalyst. The real danger to the self, from this perspective, its potentiality for fragmentation, lies

[9]In an essay in *Between Feminism and Psychoanalysis*, Moi writes, "Deconstructive logic undermines all forms of essentialism, including the Chodorovian belief in 'self-identity' or 'female identity'" (1989: 194). The French feminists are ambivalent in using "deconstructive logic" to attack the idea of a feminine identity in the sense that the discovery or recovery of the feminine occurs as a reaction to "phallocentric logic" and the history of patriarchy and "rigidity" (or reason) that has dominated and defined women. Irigaray speaks of "woman's submission by and to a culture that oppresses them, uses them, makes of them a medium of exchange, with very little profit to them. Except in the quasi monopolies of masochistic pleasure, the domestic labor force, and reproduction. The power of slaves?" (1985a: 32). The subordination of women is a "politics" enforced by the control that phallocratic reason exercises over desire. "Woman's desire has doubtless been submerged by the logic that has dominated the West since the time of the Greeks" (25). To liberate woman's desire is to define very clear boundaries between those identities framed by phallocentric structures and those self-concepts rooted in a feminine *gestalt*.

in its slippage into what Kristeva calls the "maternal abject," a state of prelinguistic confusion, a state Moi describes as "the hidden fantasies of violence and destruction linked to the pre-Oedipal mother" (1986: 11), and in which, in the boundlessness of a pretransitional object world, infantile narcissism frames the emotional conditions of psychological experience. In this psychotic state lies the "truth" of the self. Kristeva describes psychosis as "the crisis of truth in language. . . . The psychotic and the scientist bear witness (tragically for the one, optimistically for the other) to an impossible reality (1986: 218). Psychosis proceeds by the disavowal of [consensual] reality (226). [In the] economy [of psychosis] there are no *images* or *semblances* (any more than in the Eucharist): each element is neither real, nor symbolic, nor imaginary, but true" (236). And in psychosis, truth moves from the space of the word to the body itself: body becomes text. "Thus the truth of the signifier, namely, its separability, otherness, death, can be seen to be exerted on the flesh itself—as on words" (1986: 236).

Kristeva puts this notion of "truth" in a provocative context. She speaks of the "true/real," a realm of experience which contains psychosis, that space of one's being that existed before one had access to the symbolic and its structures of law and language. Moi writes, "Kristeva's argument then is that, as the true-real falls outside the framework of what is considered intelligible or plausible in the socialized space of the symbolic order, it is necessary at once to consider why this is so and what it means when the true-real actually occurs in language" (1986: 216).

I find this approach interesting, because it sounds very much like D. W. Winnicott's (1953) psychoanalytic description of the pretransitional object stage—the self's primary narcissism, its existence before it discovers the outward, expansive, and creative dimension of sociality, before its capacity to substitute or internalize the transitional object (whatever it may be, piece of blanket, stuffed animal) for the mother's presence. Lacan's notion of the "foreclosure of the father," the psychological repudiation or denial of paternal law and language, suggests that psychosis follows expulsion from the later symbolic stage and constitutes a regression to a prelinguistic, almost autistic, primitive state. Winnicott, and to a lesser extent Kristeva, would argue that psychosis signifies expulsion from the transitional embrace of the mother, who is embodied or signified or represented in the transitional object.

Kristeva, in this respect, echoes Melanie Klein as she does in much of her psychoanalytic theorizing: "I think that in the imaginary, maternal continuity is what guarantees identity" (1986: 14). Earlier, she speaks of the "maternal chora" analogous to "vocal or kinetic rhythm . . . rupture and articulations" (1974: 94). In that sense, her concept reflects Irigaray's "flow . . . fluidity" of the feminine presence, but for Kristeva the chora has a haunting, pessimistic, and depressed quality, which she calls the "abject." It is not structure; it cannot be "posited"; it is a "becoming," forever changing. It refers to a presence within the mirror of the mother's language and projections. It is a concept akin to Winnicott's notion of the holding environment, although Winnicott's concept of maternal presence is more comforting, more protective, than Kristeva's.[10]

Kristeva does argue that psychoanalysis may transform nihilism into an acceptable intellectual position; it substitutes faith in an integration of body and mind for faith in gods and ideologies. "If psychoanalytic nihilism exists, it is a nihilism that encompasses both the subjectification *and* the objectification of man's being as a creature of language viewed in terms of his relations to others: openness, consolidation, increase" (1987: 61). I am not so sure that this nihilism is possible, but postmodernism, and here I believe French philosophers such as Baudrillard and Lyotard to be representative figures,

---

[10]Winnicott places a great deal of weight on maternal presence as a guiding and therefore civilizing dynamic. He writes: "In between the infant and the object is some thing or some activity or sensation. Insofar as this joins the infant to the object (viz. maternal part-object), so far is this the basis of symbol-formation. On the other hand, insofar as this something separates instead of joins, so is its function of leading on to symbol-formation blocked (1965: 146). Further, if this process is blocked, if the transitional object fails to move the infant away from its omnipotent connection with the all-powerful mother, that failure may be traced to deficiencies in "the mother's adaptation to the infant's hallucinations and spontaneous impulses" (146). It is an adaptation that in Winnicott's terms is not "good enough" (145); the responsibility for the failure to find civil coordinates in the psychological world falls heavily on the mother. That failure may remain in the self as a split-off part self, yet retain enormous power over how consciousness experiences the surrounding world, what Winnicott calls environmental demands. "The clinical picture is one of general irritability, and of feeding and other function disturbances which may, however, disappear clinically, only to reappear in serious form at a later stage" (146). For Lacan that failure is traced to the self's inadequate internalization of law and to the power of the (precivil) Imaginary in inhibiting or preventing altogether the emergence of the self's social and linguistic functions.

advocates a virulent nihilism that goes far beyond Kristeva's muted skepticism.

For Kristeva, then, the subject is more than an ideological construct in a world of practices, power, and texts. As a psychoanalyst she demonstrates a sensitivity to the debilitating and ultimately annihilating effects of the lack of identity, the real danger of a psychotic unhinging. Winnicott describes this regression as the isolation of the pretransitional object stage (1965: 180–82), Kristeva as a return to the maternal abject, Klein as the paranoid/schizoid position (1946). The self without a firm grounding in its own subjectivity may slip toward the terrors of psychosis or massive disconnection. The civil world, Lacan's symbolic, what Winnicott calls the "social," the universe of language and otherness, situates human experience within a context that strives to forge those mechanisms whereby the self might defend itself from disintegration. Of course, it may also be the case that the symbolic, the world of law and therefore of politics, drives consciousness to distraction and madness.

Psychoanalysis and Postmodernism

What psychoanalysis is as a politics depends on which "school" one chooses to analyze, but it would be hard to imagine psychoanalysis in any of its schools, with the possible exception of the Lacanian project of decentering, to be supportive of the ends of disconnection, the break-up of the self's identity. Even Lacan would distance himself from the argument in postmodernism which assaults the connection between the presence of law and the place of the self. Without context in language and civility (what Lacan calls the Law of the Father), the self may be in danger of extinction, a falling back to the Imaginary, what Lacan calls the "foreclosure of the father." No matter how radical Lacan may be in relation to more conservative strains in main-line psychoanalysis (specifically his critique of American ego psychology), he never supports taking apart identity if that means throwing the self into a psychological terror, a regression to a "personal prehistory."

Psychoanalysis recovers the history of the self; it is an excursion into a past and into the meanings of that past. In Kristeva's view, "psychoanalysis reveals the paradoxical nature of subjectivity" (1987: 8) but that revelation depends on an ego capable of sustaining a "psychoanalysis." To be effective, a psychoanalytic encounter therefore requires a sense of constancy within oneself—not a constancy of belief or value, not the constancy of an ideological position, but a sense of identity which gives consciousness the necessary tenacity to explore the fringes of one's linguistic and emotional being. It is this sense of identity which is often shattered in human beings suffering from self-fragmentation, from a "multiplicity" that destroys the constancy of being.

Kristeva is right: "We have always been divided, separated from nature" (8). To heal that separation, to make those divisions sensible, to lift the self from the suffering induced by a disintegrating "being," involves an effort to construct a history, to discover or create a continuity in the self which might then provide the foundation for psychological birth (or rebirth). In a passage that runs counter to the postmodernist endorsement of disconnection, Kristeva writes that psychoanalysis "reestablish[es] the provisional unity of that subject and thus . . . [prepares] it for the further trials set by the life process of the passions" (9).

R. D. Laing defines this "unity" as "ontological security": "The individual . . . may experience his own being as real, alive, whole; as differentiated from the rest of the world in ordinary circumstances so clearly that his identity and autonomy are never in question; as a continuum in time; as having an inner consistency, substantiality, genuineness and worth; as spatially co-extensive with the body; and, usually, as having begun in or around birth and liable to extinction with death. He thus has a firm core of ontological security" (1978: 41–42). Ontological security preserves being; it gives the self capacity in relations with the external world: "If a position of primary ontological security has been reached, the ordinary circumstances of life do not afford a perpetual threat to one's own existence [as they do in psychosis]. If such a basis for living has not been reached, the ordinary circumstances of everyday life constitute a continual and deadly threat" (42).

Postmodernists, however, would jettison the whole concept of security. Baudrillard's "excremental culture" corrupts ontology and links consistency, substantiality, worth, and continuity to the performative demands of instrumental rationality. Rather than seek security, therefore, the truly postmodern self moves beyond reliance on structure, form, value, historical continuity and embraces flux, contingency, and acausality. If it does not, the self remains trapped by the dead matter of modernist logic. In this view (a reading of the self which takes absolutely no account of its internal status), Laing's "ontological security" becomes an ideological ploy enforcing a socially dependent conformity.

Conclusion: The Psychological Blindness of Postmodern Perception

It is no light philosophical or practical matter to call for the abolition of unitary concepts of meaning, structure, self, and causality. To court mental states that in their clinical form present horrifying situations is dangerous existentially and politically. It may lead to a glorification of nothingness, which in order to escape contingency and loneliness, induces submission to power. Indeed, the persecutory alter personalities in multiple personality disorder suggest aspects of multiple-self organization which seek out power and its force.

Postmodernism isolates the self and argues that there is nothing hidden or split off in psychological experience, nothing inaccessible to ideological explanation. The self is simply a reflection of reality or metareality or hyperreality; therefore consciousness, if it chooses, is free to deconstruct those realities and assume or internalize an infinite variety of identities. It is not so simple.

No matter how idealized the postmodern view of self, when measured against true instances of multiplicity, it is not at all clear that the postmodernists, with the exception of the French psychoanalytic feminists, take seriously the concept of harm or injury to "being." If anything, the postmodern self is a naive, malleable self, incapable of reflecting anything other than social/ideological/cultural impositions, a self constituted only by practices and power. It is a self little different from the socially constituted self of George Herbert Mead (1939); the major difference, of course, is the postmodern assertion that the self is constituted by language. Thus, the "look-

-- ing-glass" self of Charles Horton Cooley (1984) becomes in the post-modern version a "looking glass" that appears in ideological practice and linguistic patterns.

The postmodern critic or philosopher, in focusing primarily on texts and not survivors or victims, creates a highly intellectualized self, a textualized self, a self made up of letters and words, not feelings and psychological fractures. In its ideological abhorrence of psychoanalysis, the postmodernist transforms the self into a caricature, a copy of a copy of what exists around it. The actual self, the self living multiplicity (what appears in clinical reality), however, is infinitely more complicated; and the writings of Hélène Cixous, Catherine Clément, Luce Irigaray, and Julia Kristeva show how complicated it is in relation to the sources of feminine identity and the impositions of phallocratic culture.

Postmodern critics such as Foucault and Deleuze and Guattari point to severe problems in modern society. Their positions unmask serious contradictions in the social and cultural order. Foucault's epistemes do tyrannize, or in Richard Schechner's terms: epistemes are "mysteries or *sanctums*, access to which is limited to a special class of people who know the languages of the 'truth speakers.' These 'speakers' may be computers or other artificial beings, and their oracles will slowly organize themselves into a priestly caste" (1982: 99). Psychoanalysis, too, can be and has been supportive of the status quo, and in some of its incarnations terribly conservative. Understanding the dependence of power on its matrix in knowledge is crucial to dealing with imbalances and injustices in the modern world.

Psychoanalysis is not just one approach or interpretation; it is a movement, and like any movement it has its schools, splits, deviants, and apostates. Whatever one's belief, however, human beings suffer; mental illness may in fact be more than a "label"; internal psychological dislocations may be as disorienting and painful as external forms of calamity. For postmodernists to dismiss all forms of psychological suffering and psychoanalytic interpretation as consequences of perverse knowledge/power epistemes is to ignore the fact that individuals do actually suffer from conditions such as multiple personality disorder and schizophrenia. And the postmodernists sidestep the very practical question: How should society respond to such profound dislocations in being? I agree with Kristeva's observation: "Psychoanalysis and its spiritual spin-offs nonetheless still remain today a site of active dissidence in the face of an all-embracing rationality" (1986: 295).

To conclude: the voices of psychological fragmentation are more than ideological representations or the result of social practices; they come from human beings who have lived through traumas hidden from public view, whose core sense of self has been shattered by very specific actions. The languages, then, of these victims, these survivors, signifies more than reflection on ideology, practice, biophysical structure, or the decadence of modernity.

2   MULTIPLE REALITIES:
THE SUBJECT DISINTEGRATING

If all the postmodernist conception of self means is a playing at irony, then its existential and psychological theory should be understood as serving the interests of critics who understand irony and who are in fact capable of the ego-syntonic functions of a kind of textual "play." But the theory in such philosophers as Baudrillard and Lyotard is after more; the claims are not modest. The claims in fact involve discrediting the psychoanalytic distinction between fragmentation and wholeness, multiplicity and unicity, reality and delusion, truth and nothingness, ontological security and insecurity. To obliterate these distinctions, to live with the consequences of that kind of psychic deconstruction, is from a clinical perspective to throw the self into a universe of anguish and disconnection. In reality, what comes after the deconstruction of the self is tragedy. Laurie's narrative reveals that anguish.

Laurie's Multiple Realities

Disconnected selves are selves living in misery. Laurie, a twenty-five-year-old woman who has had several hospitalizations, understands herself as being on the outskirts of life, the far edge of the civil world. Technically her diagnosis is "borderline personality disorder," yet she uses what she calls her "multiple realities" to shield her from the demands of others. Laurie's multiple realities, as she described them, are more like different orders or levels of reality appearing as either momentary hallucinations or more complex delusions. These "appearances" should be distinguished from multiple personalities, since, at this point in time, Laurie understands herself in relation to these compelling orderings of reality and not in the terms of discrete alter personalities existing as disconnected selves. The *knowledge* organizing her life lies not in multiple selfhood but in the structuring effects of hallucination and delusion. To survive her terror, then, Laurie constructs alternate or multiple realities she controls and populates with images supplying those logics she required in order to live. Trapped by a hatred for the world and herself, Laurie never sees herself as participant in any community. For her, what matters lies in the internal reaches of her imagination; the external world is the place of untruth. Interestingly, about two years after I spoke with her, Laurie was readmitted to Sheppard-Pratt with the diagnosis of multiple personality disorder; I did not speak to her during her second hospitalization.

I find Laurie's description of her world useful because it provides a relatively clear introduction to the problems of living with multiplicity; further, her narrative demonstrates what Kristeva attributes to severe psychic unhinging: living and being in the "gaping hole" of "emptiness."

For Laurie, the idea or concept of a shared reality, a communal world, has no significance; she possesses no sense of common purpose, no affective alignment with the consensual world, no empathic connection with others. She refuses to accept the interconnectedness of human desire; she rejects mutual dependencies, particularly the idea of community; she sees herself as an outcast in a world she finds threatening and without meaning. What matters to Laurie is what she sees in reality; and she dismisses the observation that her perceptions may be delusional or hallucinatory. For Laurie, these organizations of reality constitute the truth of her existence; they dictate how she feels and how she acts. "I have no place here; I have no significance on the earth; I just exist." She might agree with Cixous's observation: "In my garden of hell, words are my fools. I sit upon a throne of fire and listen to my language. Truth has been" (Cixous and Clément 1986: 6).

Laurie knows herself as an isolate, without connection or meaning in the world, like Kafka's character K in *The Castle*, as Walter Benjamin describes him: "For just as K lives in the village on Castle Hill, modern man lives in his body; the body slips away from him, is hostile toward him. It may happen that a man wakes up one day and finds himself transformed into vermin. Exile—his exile—has gained control over him" (1969: 126). Laurie's psychological exile (remarkably like that of another Kafka character, Gregor Samsa in the *Metamorphosis*) rivets her identity in whatever projections occupy her mind—projections that inevitably have about them a certain delusional or psychotic quality. She understands herself as locked out of the communicable world, out of her body; she lives in a universe of disconnected moments. Nothing makes sense other than the percepts she draws from her multiple realities, fantasized truths. In Baudrillard's terms, she engages in "the radical destruction of appearances" and occupies the "black hole which engulfs the social" (1984b: 3–4).

Laurie lives in multiple realities; she creates their structure, their "existence"; she exercises dominion over their form, shape, presence; she speaks about very few of them because of the fear that if she reveals her "most important" realities (or better, fantasies) others might steal them from her. She has spoken of some of these realities:

At night sometimes I imagine nothing exists outside my room; I convince myself: beyond the door is nothing. If I were to walk out, I would just fall away into space. But then in my mind I construct reality. I build it, the hall, patients, staff, the furniture. It all becomes mine; and when I open the door and walk out onto the hall, I have this feeling of enormous satisfaction, because I know I created it; that what exists beyond my bedroom door, the very material structure, is under my control. I have power over it; I can will it into existence or out of existence, depending on how I feel!

She believes that the hospital attempts to brainwash her; that it sadistically manipulates her behavior; that staff takes pleasure in watching her suffer; that no one, either patient or staff, ever state their true intentions. She is convinced that her existence, as she puts it, mirrors the shut-up-ness of Jean-Paul Sartre's characters in *No Exit*; she suggests "there is no way out of life except by killing yourself." Occasionally she echoes the fatalism reminiscent of Friedrich Nietzsche's doctrine of the eternal return: "My consolation is that everything that has been is eternal: the sea will cast it up again" (1968: 549).

Therapy forces her unwillingly into what she calls the "mines" of her self, an exhausting process carrying with it great frustration and pain. She detaches herself from whatever experience surrounds her and withdraws into what she calls her "secret recesses," her "fantasies," what might be understood as the Augustinian "sound which is made by no language" (1962: 483). She sees her reactions to others and events to be those of a marionette or mannikin mimicking life and reality. She is like a postmodern antihero, caught in endless repetitions, or persistent mimesis, in which her productions lack any independent autonomy but are simply copies of copies. She would agree with Foucault's grim prognostic: "there remain only groundless effects, ramifications without roots, a sexuality without a sex" (1978: 151). Laurie hates life: "Other people put demands on you and make you want them and need them, but the pain of wanting and needing is too much, so you run from it and try to escape it." Or, as Sartre says in *No Exit*: "Hell is other people."

Much of the time Laurie wishes to die; her wish is openly stated; occasionally it appears as the need to disappear, to withdraw into the "deep recesses" inside herself, to hide from others, literally to die to the world. Laurie may experience herself as opaque: people "see through" her; under these glances she feels naked. Or she "disappears" by leaving her body and psychically inhabiting a distant place. Although she seems fascinated by spiritual death, her despair over the demands of living push her into periodic contemplations of suicide, believing that she "might be better off" without her body. She comforts herself with the thought of being a desubstantiated spirit moving in other worlds. When she is in these frames of mind, death is understood as the most direct response to what she sees as the uselessness and futility of life, the lack of warmth in the universe.

Isolation defines the structure of Laurie's being; it determines the nature of her beliefs; it creates whatever meaning she finds in action. Or, in Barthes's terms:"I shall look away, that will henceforth be my sole negation" (1975: 3). Isolation gives her relief from the gaze of the other, a relief often enhanced by a variety of street drugs.

I leave the hospital [to attend classes at a local college] and no one here [Sheppard] can possibly guess what goes through my mind, what is in "there." No single person understands me; it's impossible; how can anyone else understand your feelings? . . . You're completely alone, locked away without any feeling, any faith in communication. When I go to school, I sit far back in the lecture hall so no one will look at me. I can't stand the stares; yet I have this sense that when students walk down the aisle they see right through me. . . .

Even if I tell persons what I'm feeling and thinking I'm afraid they'll take it from me; they want to steal my uniqueness and won't give it back. That's why I'll only do art therapy, alone, with the art therapist. If another patient sees my work, I know they'll use my drawings. And then it won't be mine anymore. It'll be part of them. So why even relate to people since all they want to do anyway is steal part of your self. Why subject yourself to that kind of pain? Why tell people who you are; they only want you for themselves, to take from you; they have no real desire to get to know you, to be your friend. Besides, why should people want to know me? If they did, the knowledge might poison them.

Laurie speaks of herself as a "thing that thinks," a modern rendition of a deconstructed self, literally doubting herself (and her body) into fragmented bits, in an effort to become as substance-less as possible. She experiences her body as cut off from humankind, as an object others find disgusting, beyond recognizable human shape, deserving of torture and dismemberment. She is convinced that an omnipotent fate has condemned her to live alone, to "die a quick death . . . put in the ground and forgotten." She will be, like Barthes's "disembodied eye," sucked away, vanished, drained of all being.

It is difficult, if not impossible, for Laurie to experience any pleasure; the sensations of the world degenerate into unwanted intrusions, despised presences. Nor does she see any redemptive quality in association and friendship; others intend to manipulate, use, and degrade. She feels that she is always "falling apart," disintegrating; life tears at her flesh, rips her into unrecognizable shards. She is Foucault's "bad infinity," a being without ground, a product of endless spirals of power which use her as an object and then leave her to wither and die.

Laurie occasionally recalls images from a frightening past, an earlier world of cruelty and neglect, memories of a hurt, wounded child, a yearning for unrealized connection and warmth. She suffers the gaze of a vast emptiness that, if ever recognizable, brings only the images of pain.

When I was a kid and would get upset my mother sent messages not to get upset, to keep it hidden. The messages were not direct; rather she became angry. She gave me a sense I had become a burden, and that made me terribly frightened and terribly responsible for her feelings. If my mother couldn't hold it together, if I had to try to make her feel good by not telling her how I felt, how could I possibly keep myself intact? She handled my discomfort, my crankiness, by turning off her feelings. It was like she turned to stone or ice; or when she wasn't like that, she seemed so worried I feared for her life! She went away from me . . . I mean her emotions just weren't there; she seemed to be somewhere else. Then she would get angry for no reason at all; sudden outbursts, she started yelling, and I had no idea what was going on. I thought she became upset because of something I did, but I couldn't figure it out.

Her anger terrified me. So what I did was set up in my mind a kind of perfect non-angry happy Laurie. I could meet my mother's expectations by not getting myself agitated or upset. It was an ingenious solution. I never told her when I felt bad; I never asked for any comfort. If I hid my feelings by literally forcing myself to believe I wasn't upset or angry, then I wouldn't bother my mother. Nor would I need her warmth, affection, care. I handled it alone, tearing out of myself the hurt and storing it up somewhere inside where it wouldn't affect me. I learned how to make myself invisible.

At the same time, I could be what my mother wanted me to be: a happy go-lucky child showing all the outward signs of a well-adjusted kid. Yet I didn't realize at the time that the act went

against my grain, how terrible I felt. Yet I convinced myself I had
to do this to survive; I even convinced myself I actually was
happy. But the pressure built up intense feelings: one moment
I was angry, another in tears. It has been going on for years.

My parents never knew. As far as they were concerned I was a
good kid, doing well in school, bringing home good grades, dating,
things like that. After a while, I even lost touch with how I felt,
with the despair, unhappiness. I believed their stories about how
good I was, how happy, and how they were so lucky to have such
a healthy child, how I made them proud . . . all that stuff. Yet
something inside seemed to bother me, I felt a need to escape. So I
turned to drugs very early (I guess I was fourteen or fifteen) to escape the pressure, the tension. I thought I would crack into a mil-
lion pieces; it got worse after the drugs wore off. Then I really felt
the depression, its heaviness. It was like being oppressive to myself; I hated being who I was! I needed to run away from my body,
to become light, lighter than air. It got bad, but my abortion [when
she was twenty-one] blew away all my illusions. Depression came,
barreling into me like a ten-ton truck; a few weeks later I tried to
kill myself.

Unable to feel empathy from her surrounding world, sensing a
deprivation that intensified as she grew older, desperately attempting to escape despair through drugs, Laurie finds herself oscillating
between periodic narcissistic rages (a radical frustration in being)
and overwhelming sensations of being bad, dirty, and corrupt. Who
she is as a person, her identity, resonates massive "cracks" in her
being. Her values, then, her attitudes toward persons and experience, the metaphors she chooses to define her identity, her selfhood
(her individuality), reflect this shattered internal sense of being: "ugliness like blood runs through my veins . . . my insides are twisted
and poisoned; someone should come right in here and twist my
head off."

Or, in Cixous's words: "I'm afraid to hear myself speak.—What
have you done?—I have known death.—Be frank.—Death has
known me.—Be frank.—I have made love with death. How I wish
there was nothing left! When will I be acquitted? Will I never be at
Peace? It is no use carrying away the corpse, imprisoning it in its
sarcophagus—the empty room is filled with death" (1985: 111).

Laurie's Existence in Fantasy: Multiple Realities as Epistemological Framework

Laurie surrounds her perceptual life with what Heinz Kohut calls "frightening, shameful and isolating narcissistic fantasies," resistances that prevent the self from using "insight as a stepping stone toward realistic action" (1971: 150). Hers is a fantasy world structured as bipolar oppositions: she oscillates between identification with her grandiose self (self as perfect, beyond the need to communicate with others, all-knowing, all-powerful) and disintegrated self (self as slime, the lowest of the low, the scum of the earth). Fantasy then (or multiple realities) composes each pole of the opposition: the conviction of absolute perfection and specialness or the belief that she occupies the body of a horribly deformed creature who provokes disgust.

In her inner world, therefore, Laurie moves from one pole of her multiple realities to the other without relief, comfort, or hope: the power to control versus the feeling of being out of control; unattainable expectations, the drive for perfection versus the feeling of being utterly worthless, without any capacities; the knowledge of being better than everyone else, powerful, beyond human in intellectual achievement, versus the feeling of being dirt, dung, or garbage. Nothing in between these poles (ambivalent experience, feeling, orientations) matters, because for Laurie existential purpose consists only in "eating and passing your genes onto the next generation." It is nothing more than that, a dreary procession of actions without pleasure or meaning, just enough energy expended and sustenance ingested to stay alive, to avoid killing oneself. Limitation, imperfection, subtle mediations, for example, between power and control, and letting oneself be controlled, nothing of the ambivalent in hu-

Grandiose	*Disintegrated*
absolute	slime, scum
perfection beyond being human	deathlike emptiness
no need for others	malevolent, paranoid world
	experience as terror

Figure 1 Oppositions in Laurie's self-structure

man relationship enters into Laurie's consciousness. Her frame of reference depends entirely on terms established by radical antimonies, a relentless internal movement, skidding between identification with power and greatness and the knowledge of self as worthless. It is a process of living which takes place in isolation; and whatever form these multiple realities take, they play themselves out, for the most part, without witness, without others, without any mirroring from the consensual universe. The real action, then, of Laurie's being lies in the hidden, private reaches of her fantasy formations; and in this disembodied, emotional hermitage so at odds with Laurie's cognitive sophistication, she unravels and lives out the structure of her existence and the significance she attaches to it.

Laurie's frequent outbursts of anger also buttress her narcissistic fantasies; anger, symptomatic of an inner panic that provokes extreme anxiety, defends against the fear of being destroyed or invaded by the other. Anger functions as a desperate maneuver to preserve psychological boundary, to maintain the very fluid distinction between self and Other; it inhibits the creation of any idealizing transference. And pushing the Other away by making oneself as unpleasant as possible not only protects the self from exposure and intimacy, it also intensifies and expands the fantasy formations.

If the external world appears as filled with evil and danger, it is safer to be or dwell inside, to withdraw into multiple realities that, while frightening, present a different order of threat than does the external world. At least on the inside, Laurie need not fear dissolution and disappearance, since fantasy, Kristeva's "psychotic text," functions as the Other. Although anger creates a negativistic and hostile connection between self and Other, for Laurie its central function lies in distancing, in reinforcing the internal coordinates of her being and in preserving her from the threat of identity dissolution and spiritual annihilation. In addition, anger effectively erodes trust relations, particularly when the self's concept of trust possesses archaic qualities. Laurie's sense of trust runs something like the following: "Do what I want, when I want, and let me exist in whatever reality I choose to construct or deconstruct. If you let me be like this, then I'll trust you." Only an omnipotent idealized mother could gratify such an unlimited sense of entitlement.

Disintegrated (Laurie)	Integrated (cohesive or nuclear self)
Self-hatred	Self-esteem, stable social values
Worthlessness	Self-worth limited and modulated by consensual reality
Unlimited rage, fury, as effort to defend against intimacy	Appropriately controlled anger; assimilation and integration of "archaic selfobject"
Multiple realities (fragmented selfobject representations)	Acceptance of consensual reality; idealizations integrated into self-structure
Sense of emotional world as dead and ungiving, as unforgiving and cold	Emotional world as joyful, embodied, and real
Need and demand to be perfect	Acceptance of limitation, imperfection; socially modulated sense of efficacy
Need to be "not there" as a self, to replace existent self with fantasized self	Need to be "there," cooperating with and learning from others; distinct sense of self/not self
Will "not to be"	Will to "be"; creativity, productivity, skills, tasks, humor, and wisdom

Figure 2 Disintegrated versus integrated self-structure

Figure 2 looks at elements in Laurie's disintegrated self against properties Kohut would assign to the integrated cohesive self.

Self-disintegration leads to massive distortions in reality perception; nothing is what it seems. A dramatic instance of this process in Laurie appears in what she "experiences" on her walk to her college class, in the classroom itself, and on the return to the hospital—a terrifying series of events involving various multiple realities. On her way to class, Laurie believes that all people who walk by her wish to hurt her; every step requires constant vigilance and persistent monitoring. Passing strangers want to rape and kidnap her; they hide torture devices to be used after her capture; they plan to take her to a distant part of the city.

In the classroom itself, she believes students look at her with the intent of figuring out ways to hurt her after class; she knows several students plot to attack and then mutilate her as she walks back to Sheppard-Pratt. Further, she believes that the instructor (while lecturing) sends symbolic, telekinetic messages about death, destruction, and sexual perversion. And his lectures disguise his real intent, which is to draw Laurie into perversity and degradation. If any students were to come to know her, either by striking up a chance conversation or over a cup of coffee after class, they would become disgusted; repulsed by what they saw, they would immediately round up friends to do horrible things to her body, an act consistent with her belief that "life is punishment." Even if she were to meet some classmates on her way back, just for a moment, they would "see through" her and be shocked at the revelations. She feels "shame" at what they might discover and feels "exposed" in the lecture hall; "I want to leave; I want to get out of there as quick as possible; but I make myself quiet and still, small, so I will become invisible and no one will see me; that's how I make it through class."

Once she returns to the safety of Sheppard's grounds, the disconnected fragments of terror remain, but they shift: their focus now is on different scenarios, people, and stories. The dread of being attacked, the fear of exposure and shame, the knowledge of her poisonousness become permanent fixtures in her imagination and spin off more horrifying multiple worlds.

One additional observation directly comments on Laurie's intense fear in revealing any of her multiple realities that she regards as "shameful" and "disgusting," her need to resist so strenuously the sharing of beliefs and feelings. If Laurie were to share her secrets, and by this she means those secrets that contain the most "shameful" aspects of who she knows herself to be, she would become, through this act of reciprocity, a Siamese twin with the shared Other. She would become Other, and the Other would fuse into self. She would then find herself attached but in such a way that, because of the threat to her identity, she would be compelled to "detach" herself. Yet detaching from her "twin" would involve violent action. Think of it, she argues, as analogous to what might be required to separate, physically, Siamese twins. If both twins share the same organs, one twin obviously has to be sacrificed, otherwise the act of separation would mutilate the heart, liver, lungs, kidneys, and so on; both would die. Sharing organs is therefore physiologically impossible. A choice has to be made: one of the twins dies. Laurie identifies with the twin who would have to be killed.

The extent to which Laurie applies this analogy to herself in all cases of revealing her multiplicity is unclear. Yet she insists she possesses "secrets" she never will reveal; it is too threatening, too much of a danger to her identity. The prospect of sharing terrifies her because she is convinced that the other intends to appropriate her being; and she could be separated only through a violent ripping that would mean her death. Keeping secrets inside, then, denying reciprocity and sharing in favor of isolation, hermetic withdrawal, and grandiose fantasies, becomes, paradoxically, a defense against death, because to share means annihilation of self.

The psychological costs of this isolation are enormous. Not only does Laurie's emotional hermitage inhibit specific therapeutic benefits (demystifying fantasy), but the retaining of secrets prolongs her pain, her wish for a physical death, the anguish of her existence, and the stream of multiple realities that provide her with "pieces" of an identity. The tormenting fantasy worlds haunt her consciousness and keep her in a state of psychological servitude to archaic self-objects whose resolution is essential if she is to pursue any kind of fulfilling life, if she is to discover the experience of pleasure, as opposed to the distraction and terror of escape. For Laurie, then, Sartre's *No Exit* might serve as a compelling metaphor for existence.

The Distortion of Transference
Relationships in Laurie's Multiple Realities

The psychotic self rejects becoming for permanent isolation, as Winnicott writes: "[T]he non-communicating central self, for ever immune from the reality principle," remains in psychosis "for ever silent" (1965: 192). This disconnected self, without community, polity, or language, lacks an internal ground or being experienced as whole, safe, and protected. Although Laurie was not in a technical sense psychotic, she suffered from psychotic or delusional moments that defined her day-to-day life and the epistemology she used to organize experience.

The self that exists emotionally in a psychotic space, an equivalent to the narcissistic internality of infancy, has not traversed the bridge between inner and other. The psychotic self suffers from what Winnicott calls a "failure of basic provision," a radical lack or emptiness he traces to the dialectic between mother and infant. What Cixous describes as the "song of the mother" has been silenced in psychosis. Consciousness is afflicted by a depleted, crippled core, an ahistoricity dominated by delusional projections and fears of imminent annihilation. Such selves have relinquished being; what exists inside, in fantasy, which for the infant is the world, lacks all sense of trust and coherence. Psychosis, as I have noted, has an entirely different origin for Lacan, deriving from the "foreclosure" of paternal law. Lacan's lack of interest in maternal failure and his view of the mother as a kind of conduit, in the mirror stage, for social signifiers—which are themselves products of the *paternally* defined "symbolic"—is a serious limitation in his approach to psychotic disintegration.

Persons in psychosis make efforts to preserve those shreds or fragments of self that remain, to protect the cut-off core of the inner self, and to ward off "the threat of its being found, altered, communicated with" (Winnicott 1965: 187). For the psychotic self, desperately protecting its core (feelings of aliveness or deadness, being or nonbeing), any form of communication "seeping through the defenses" (187) holds life-threatening possibilities. The knowledge system of psychosis, or delusion, protects this terrified core from contact, interpersonal exchange, social communication, and the trust necessary for life in community. It also poses special problems in the psychoanalytic transference relationship.

The psychoanalytic relationship allows for the representation of early infantile distortions. I shall briefly comment on this relationship because it illuminates how Laurie's multiplicity or multiple realities distort the whole fabric of human relationships; in the transference Laurie's internal projections become a source not only of torment but of a series of defenses against relationship.[1]

---

[1]Regarding transferences with multiple personality patients, Judith Herman writes: "The patient with multiple personality disorder represents the extreme in the complications of traumatic transference. The transference may be highly fragmented, with different components carried by different alters. . . . Therapists working with these patients [should] prepare for intensely hostile and sexualized transferences as a matter of routine. . . . The emotional vicissitudes of the recovery relationship are therefore bound to be unpredictable and confusing for patient and therapist alike" (1992: 140). Further, "it is not uncommon for experienced therapists to feel suddenly incompetent and hopeless in the face of a trau-

Kohut argues that the psychoanalytic relation restores through the different transferences the course of what he calls "gradual modification" to the infantile "grandiose self," a process that is "traumatically interrupted in childhood" (1971: 108). It enables the self to refract its injuries, to visualize their structure partly through the activation of fantasy, to assimilate infantile sensations of entitlement, unexplainable anxiety, and frustration.

He elaborates three kinds of transference relationships established by the "grandiose self" with surrounding objects. Each transference (merger, twinship or alter ego, mirror) is experienced in different forms and with varied actors throughout life, although it is most intensely felt and reacted to in infancy and childhood, and most dramatically recreated in the psychoanalytic relation.

Kohut uses these terms as follows. *Merger*: the integration of the grandiose self is facilitated by the self's capacity both to merge with the other, or object, and to separate from it. Each of these actions, merger and separation, frames the self's narcissistic aims. In the merger transference, "the relationship to the analyst is one of (primary) identity" (114). *Twinship*: strengthening the self depends on the ability to utilize omnipotent objects as a "twin" or "alter ego," to learn from this kind of relation, to move beyond it, to deidealize the parental *imago*, yet at the same time retain respect and trust. "[T]he narcissistically cathected object is experienced as being like the grandiose self or as being very similar to it" (115), while "the patient assumes that the analyst is either like him or similar to him, or that the analyst's psychological makeup is like, or is similar to, that of the patient" (115). *Mirror*: to rely on the other as a "mirror for the essential human needs of echoing, confirming, and accepting" enhances the self's sense of its own capacities and provides the foundation for realistic self esteem. The mirror transference reflects "the child's exhibitionist display and other forms of maternal participation and response to the child's narcissistically exhibitionistic enjoy-

---

matized patient" (141). And "additional complications of countertransference are to be expected with patients who have a complex post-traumatic syndrome. Especially with survivors of prolonged, repeated abuse in childhood, the therapist may initially respond more to the damaged relational style of the survivor than to the trauma itself" (146).

ment." Further, effective mirroring "confirms the child's self esteem, and, by a gradually increasing selectivity of the responses, begins to channel it into realistic directions" (116–17). It is as if the analyst and the "archaic selfobject" occupy the same psychological space: "As was the mother during that state of development, so is now the analyst an object which is important only insofar as it is invited to participate in the child's narcissistic pleasure and then to confirm it . . . echoing, approving, and confirming plays a central role in the working through process" (116–17).

Kohut would agree with Winnicott's observation that "The precursor of the mirror is the mother's face" (1982: 111). And the mother provides a vital, identity-creating "environmental provision." For Kohut the mirror stage enhances the self's integrity; it gives it strength; for Lacan, however, the mirror stage introduces an alienation so profound that the ego finds itself founded on "misrecognition." Lacan's concept of the mirror, therefore, is considerably more pessimistic than Kohut's.

Each of these "transferences" contributes to the self's emerging individuality; each adds to the self's sense of its own capacities; each refracts and limits the self's omnipotent identification and unlimited sense of entitlement. And each brackets the developmental process.[2] But most important for our purposes, it is the transference that allows the therapist or analyst to witness (and discover the meaning behind) the nature of the self's transformations, the core of its subjectivity and the direction of its multiplicity. Multiple realities, multiple selves—each appears within the context of these transferences, or in the case of schizophrenia, its fragmentation. What Kristeva calls "the whole symbolic matrix sheltering emptiness," with its terrifying confusion, defines the linguistic field of the transference (1986: 245).

With Laurie, each of these relations has been frustrated, inhibited, and broken up; as she puts it, she "uses" her multiple realities (her fantasy formations) as defenses against establishing a durable

---

[2]Compare with Kohut's critique of traditional interpretations of the oedipus complex: "The dramatic conflict-ridden Oedipus complex of classical analyses, with its perception of a child whose aspirations are crumbling under the impact of castration fear, is not a primary maturational necessity but only the frequent result of frequently occurring failures from the side of narcissistically disturbed parents" (1977: 247).

or trusting relation with her therapist. She therefore desperately re-sists exploring any of the manifestations of an internal self which constantly frustrate her efforts to be in the world. Laurie cannot move in and out of merger relationships; to become too close to any other means annihilation of identity (she would literally forget who she is). She believes that the other, notably her therapist, would steal, appropriate, or otherwise eliminate her being. "When I sat with Dr. _____ I thought I might die; occasionally I saw 'Death' sitting on top of Dr. _____'s head."

Nor does she find any comfort in the idea that some other out there might be like her or might function as an alter ego; in Laurie's view of the world, each self is distinct and inviolable. It is therefore absurd to imagine any similarity and identity, much less commu-nity. For example, if she shares her secrets (her inner self, her fanta-sies), she puts herself in danger of becoming the other's Siamese twin. She finds the prospect that an alter ego might teach her some-thing in the way of values, as against the knowledge contained in her "secrets" or multiple realities, to be repugnant and frightening.

Laurie's perspective here is quite "postmodern": teaching in the realm of values is, in her view, impossible, because nothing in soci-ety deserves to be emulated. Everything is repetition, copy; manipu-lation of image lies behind all forms of social experience. Teachers, wherever they exist, provide information, nothing more; they are literally information machines. Mirroring remains outside Laurie's experience because "echoing, confirming, and accepting" constitute "hypocrisies." The only reality that confirms anything is the reality of her image of the world as a dreadful place, and the imminence of death.[3] The external world is concerned only with using human en-ergy for domination, profit, and torture.

Laurie shows little delight in being "exhibitionistic." Rather, she

---

[3]The "realities" (and wishes) of borderline patients can be violent; for example, Alex-andra, a twenty-one-year-old woman, believes that her boyfriend loves her so much that if she were attracted to another man, and he found her with the other man in a burning barn, he would let her die before acknowledging or accepting the fact of her being with someone else. Alexandra also periodically has the fantasy that if she found herself trapped in a burning barn her boyfriend, on the way to rescue her, would be killed and mutilated in a car accident. Her artwork often reflected these themes, yet she could also draw faces of great sensitivity, extraordinary suffering, the images of despair, resignation, and hopeless-ness. I am indebted to Dr. Sally Winston for this example.

intends to keep these "mirroring" mechanisms inside, to engage in self/self dialogue, with her fantasies or secrets as the "mirror." In Lacanian terms, if the Imaginary functions as mirror, if it displaces the symbolic (that is, the civil world), the self exists in a psychotic state. Self/other discourse externalizes fantasy, demystifies its power, and establishes the social context for oedipal conflict.

To mirror effectively requires an existence firmly rooted in the symbolic/linguistic world; in that respect, what is consensual is what the social world accepts as symbolic. Laurie rejects consensual understandings, the public quality or character of the symbolic and its accompanying law. For her, then, confirmation of self lies not in what is socially or even linguistically sanctioned, but what the imagination produces as meaning and truth. Her multiple realities take her away from social forms and leave her in a state of interpersonal immobility and terror.

Kristeva examines this concept of psychological truth not as a logical or ontological property but as an aspect of the self which is mad. The true is the "unnameable" part of one's self. It is also what is most "real," in the sense that it underlies all identity. The "true/real" therefore derives from a primitive unconscious, in Lacanian terms, a presymbolic universe that contains archaic part-objects filled with memory traces. In adults, for example in Laurie, those memory traces, composites of unconscious fantasies and repressed desire, appear as the truth of the "psychotic text" (1986b: 218) or the reality of madness. To be psychotic, then, is to live in the realm of the "true/real": the immanence of madness, a massive regression to a precivil psychological space.

The key to understanding Laurie's subjectivity or multiplicity lies in an examination of these transference relations as literal forms of experience, as actions in a continuing process of resolution. It is precisely this resolution and its almost Hegelian property of moving the self toward increasingly higher levels of spiritual and psychological integration which is missing in Laurie, because effective resolution of the transferences anchors the self in an ontology that possesses consensual meaning and involves others. Laurie's unconscious project lay in running from this "value"; her affirmation of nihilism is the desperate maneuver she undertakes to protect her from persons, specifically from the actions of trusting and loving. Laurie, therefore, subverts the transference at every opportunity; she will have none of its "reason," its search for meaning. She would rather draw her existential categories from the truth hidden in her multiple realities.

Although Laurie shows remarkable sophistication and presence in defending her views intellectually, it is too threatening for her, beyond her affective range, to acknowledge the transferences as lived realities, much less to examine and experience their implications emotionally. If she were capable of transference in Kohut's terms, she might use the therapist [in the merger] "as an extension of [her] own (split-off and/or repressed) archaic greatness and exhibitionism"; or she might experience "him (in the alter ego transference) as the separate carrier of [her] own (repressed) perfection"; or she might demand "from him (in the mirror transference) an echo and a confirmation of [her] greatness and an approving response to [her] exhibitionism" (1971: 123). Laurie undertakes none of these actions.

Further, if she, again in Kohut's terms, were a patient capable of utilizing transference, she might use the therapeutic relationship as a "buffer," allowing her to demystify fantasy structures, thereby enabling the "modification" of the grandiose self, and the achievement of "firmly established object-directed strivings" (145). Kohut says that: "the main therapeutic benefit which accrues from the transference like condition established by the activation of the grandiose self is that it enables the patient to mobilize and maintain a working-through process in which the analyst serves as a therapeutic buffer and enhances the gradual harnessing of the ego alien narcissistic fantasies and impulses" (123). Laurie, however, refuses this connection and strives, valiantly, to maintain her solipsistic terror; her very real disintegration anxiety derives from the ontological status she grants to her multiple realities. In this Kafkian world of terrorized solitude, with its hermetically sealed realities, its language of fantasy and self/self discourse, Laurie waits, like Samuel Beckett's Godot, enduring her physical body as the last impediment to liberation, the final humiliation.

Conclusion: Laurie's Postmodernist Self?

Laurie's persistent delusional identifications, her distrust of the shared world, her retreat to interior psychological spaces, her regression, signify a self that has yet to consent to participate in a consensually defined world. In a literal sense, Laurie's affective self remains outside the polity, outside of time and therefore history. Her desires derive from a multiplicity that possesses a delusional substrate; her private knowledge system remains the form of experience she finds familiar. Demands from the consensual world, the emotional greed of others, Laurie cannot tolerate; when she confronts this kind of externality, her consciousness shatters, her sense of connection disintegrates, and she finds herself in multiple realities that from the outside looking in appear to be mad. Periodically, Laurie engages in social rituals, but emotionally she lives in another universe, "the unnamed fears that belong to the unreachable" (Winnicott 1971: 120), not in the world of shared illusion, but in one of hermetic isolation.

Laurie lives the disconnected reality of postmodernism, but it is a tragic condition; her disconnection brings total incapacity. She exists in the world not as a sentient human being engaged with others but as a consciousness desperately struggling with fragmentation. Without a historic identity, an identity rooted in psychodevelopmental time that possesses a continuity, Laurie's self falls apart; her multiple realities coalesce as a delusional knowledge structure. Whatever safety appears to consciousness Laurie finds in this terrifying isolation, with its immobilizing images. Cixous's image describes this terror: "Despite my buzzing noises, a hand tears off my legs, a hand rips off my wings, the pain does not kill me, the body shrivels up; and outside the window there's no ground to lie crushed on. And my two wings torn off" (1985: 9). For Laurie this kind of ripping, self-violence defines the fragments of her self. Hers is not a liberating or playful experience; her multiple realities annihilate the self's emotional possibility, destroy the psychological foundations of consent, and shatter the shared experiences of historical knowledge.

3 MULTIPLE PERSONALITIES: TERROR IN A PRECIVIL PSYCHOLOGICAL SPACE

I became interested in the psychiatric diagnosis of multiple personality disorder because it seemed both bizarre and real: bizarre in the sense that it is difficult to grasp what it means to live with several different personalities inhabiting one's body, and real in the sense that the switching of personalities I observed appeared compelling and the narratives about abuse, horrendous. I was struck by the increasing numbers of women entering the hospital with this diagnosis and by the sheer brutality of the experience itself. I found it almost impossible to believe that fathers could do what the patients described to me: that small children, even babies, could be victimized, tortured, raped, violated without any regard for the integrity of their bodies.

Psychiatrists argue among themselves over the sudden interest in the diagnosis: what it means, why it had been dormant for so many years, why suddenly in the 1980s the appearance of women with multiple personality disorder should dramatically rise as populations within mental hospitals and as patients in therapists' offices. There are a number of explanatory factors: the general suspicion of the diagnostic cluster in psychiatry historically; the classification of such women under the borderline category; the lack of knowledge about the diagnosis in both psychiatry and psychoanalysis; the rise of interest in traumatic stress disorders, and the psychological phenomenon of dissociation (a spillover from the ex-

perience of Vietnam veterans); the increase in the reporting of childhood and sexual abuse among women; the influence of feminist literature and politics in focusing professional interest on woman as
victim (Mitchell 1984) and renewed interest in the seduction theory
Freud abandoned prior to the publication of *The Interpretation of
Dreams* (Masson 1984).

➤ Many in the medical psychiatric world remain hostile to the diagnosis; N. Humphrey and D. C. Dennett argue that some see it as
"scientifically or philosophically absurd. . . . It is considered to be
unsupported by objective evidence. . . . It is considered to be an
iatrogenic folly." I would agree that "the syndrome is a real one
nonetheless." Yet the controversy surrounding the diagnosis is in
large measure intensified by the "cliquish, almost cultish character
of those who currently espouse the cause of MPD. In a world where
those who are not for MPD are against it, it is perhaps not surprising that 'believers' have tended to close ranks" (1989: 92–93). The
diagnosis, then, has about it a knowledge/power debate and struggle within the profession of psychiatry, a political argument over
classification and nosology and in Foucault's terms, the politics of
disciplines and "domains" (1977: 194).

Role versus Identity

Clinical cases demonstrate that the multiple "roles" one plays in
society possess a much different meaning from that of multiple identities, and the two ought not to be confused. The postmodernists (as
opposed to the psychoanalytic feminists) use the word "identity" in
a way that makes it synonymous with role function. An *identity* lo-
cates the self in the world; it defines emotional and interpersonal
knowledge; it frames the self in a historical and situational context.
A *role*, however, is what the self does; roles comment on how the
self appears, the tasks it masters. To have multiple identities is to
have a self without any center, any sense of its own history and
place in a definable community, family, and polity. It is a terrible
mistake, in a psychological sense, to think that multiple roles or interests or tastes define a multiple self; the multiple personality suffers from an indeterminate number of identities whose origins have

nothing to do with the role functions of culture or with specific techniques required to master roles (Beahrs 1982; Bliss 1986; Smith et al. 1982).

The multiple personality lives in a world of utter confusion. No single self defines 'being.' "How can I ever know who I am, if whoever I am is one of the many inside me?" is how one patient put it. "I can never know who is out, because I have no memory of any alter ever being out." But when Jane or Mary or Lizzie or "girl" or "child" or "rage" is out, the host personality has absolutely no recollection of their presence or their action. Other people may say to her, "You were acting differently," or, "You kept saying your name was Mary," and so on. The self (the host self) has absolutely no control over who she is, or any historical memory of her different manifestations.

The postmodernist attack on unicity (the unitary, rational self) raises problems, particularly around the notion of a cohesive self-identity existing independently of roles, social alliances, meta-discourses defining the subject. In this respect, psychoanalytic object-relations theorists such as Winnicott, Fairbairn, Harry Guntrip, and Otto Kernberg suggest a significant critique of postmodernism's celebration of multiplicity. It should be noted, however, that object-relations theory with its clinical backdrop, its empirical foundation in the experience of the self, and its concept of, if not a unitary, at least a cohesive self moves against several arguments in postmodernism.

Clinical Approaches to Multiple Personalities

The *Diagnostic and Statistical Manual of the American Psychiatric Association*, third edition, revised, defines the diagnostic criteria for multiple personality disorder: "A. The existence within the person of two or more distinct personalities or personality states (each with its own relatively enduring pattern of perceiving, relating to, and thinking about the environment and self). B. At least two of these personality or personality states recurrently take full control of the person's behavior" (272).

It has been estimated that 97 percent of persons who receive the diagnosis of multiple personality disorder have suffered a history of prolonged child abuse, including a history of severe sexual abuse beginning in childhood (Putnam 1989; Shengold 1989). Nine out of ten people seen in clinical settings with this diagnosis are women (Putnam et al. 1986; Ross, Norton, and Wozneys 1989). Pierre Janet (1907), who discovered the syndrome, characterized it as a "trance state disorder." (For an early description of the phenomenon, see Prince 1906).

Patients describe having shifting identities as an existence lacking stability and a fixed orientation as to time and space (Baldwin 1984). Nothing is identifiable as essential or historically consistent in the self (Crabtree 1985; Hawthorn 1983). No one moment of identity, not even the host personality, appears dominant. "It is as if certain groups of personalities overlie each other or are buried beneath other personalities" (Putnam 1989: 124). Personalities may switch quite rapidly or engage in debate which the host personality silently mediates. Personalities may appear as layered: "The experience of working with layering," Putnam argues, "with its levels within levels, within levels of complexity, may leave the therapist feeling frustrated and wondering whether it will ever end." Layering, however, defends against remembrance. "Layering phenomena . . . are just part of the defensive process of dissociation that binds pain and horror by dividing it into little parts and storing it in such a way that it is difficult to reassemble and to remember" (125).

Such multiplicity torments the "host personality," who often suffers the "remembering" or flashbacks initiating the journey into the truth of the self. An alter may give to the host personality the function of remembering, or the host may designate a certain alter as the agent who holds the pain or its memories. In R. P. Kluft's view, "the therapist refuses to take sides with any of the personalities but opposes any efforts of any to do harm to themselves, and other personalities, the body, or other individuals" (1984: 16). Putnam writes, "The diagnosis of MPD is often a liberating event for multiples, who have practiced deception and secrecy as a way of life. Alters are now overly eager to separate themselves from the host personality, who is usually perceived as pathetic and incompetent" (1989: 132).

To recollect trauma is to open cracks in the alter compartments such that each alter may speak to or address others. Some patients describe the process as "lifting the fog" or "getting everyone into a room" and [from the therapist's perspective] gradually bringing that room into sharper and sharper focus, to the point where alters begin to resemble other alters or the room becomes smaller and smaller as therapy proceeds. Some therapists argue that because so much damage was done at such an early age, the "remembering" of trauma initiates a process whereby a self may be consolidated, primitive affects brought into view, and language used to firm up a central self no longer relating to experience as an endless flight from terror.

Alter personalities embody many different affects and experiences. "All personalities," however, E. L. Bliss argues, "begins as friends and allies, or if you will, invited guests." Some friends and allies may turn into enemies; others may be "amicable" or bring "confidence." Others may be "macabre, bent on assault, suicide and homicide." He continues, "The personalities may appear only once for a single mission and thereafter remain dormant, or they may continue to function either as shadowy, unconscious influences or as a dominant force when they periodically take over the body. One personality assumed control of the body for an entire year, leaving the patient with an amnesia for that period" (1986: 131).

Psychoanalytically, the presence of alters has been formulated as a collection of introjects, each with an autonomous personality structure. Roy Schaefer describes the introject as "an inner presence with which one feels in a continuous or intermittent dynamic relationship. The subject conceives of this presence as a person, a physical or psychological part of a person . . . or a person-like thing or creature. He experiences it as existing within the confines of his body or mind or both, but not as an aspect or expression of his subjective self. The topographic quality of this internal presence may be unconscious, preconscious or conscious, and it may change" (1968: 72).

R. P. Horevitz and B. G. Braun see the host personality as "extremely depleted of reserves, anxious, helpless and hopeless, victimized, frequently depressed to the point of paralysis" (1984: 81). Other commentators raise questions about the reliability of the host personality and think the "host" may be a series of ever-changing alters. Therapists working with multiples find that during the consolidation of the self the host personality may undergo significant transformation. What, over time, replaces her presence is a self with

a greater affective and expressive range drawn from the various alters. Memory in addition comes to be more completely shared. Putnam states that "in a multiple, the memory of a traumatic experience
may be contained within a single alter, or it may be spread across
several alters. When a memory is divided among several alters, each
alter may contain a fragment of the event, or one alter may contain
the memory for the details of the event while others hold the affects
generated by the event. It is the therapist's job to help the patient
reassemble the whole memory" (1989: 198–99).

Origins of Multiple Personality

For the multiple personality, as for the psychotic, what Winnicott
calls "environmental provision" has been a total disaster. Technically, multiple personalities are not psychotic. Protection of a traumatized and violated core takes the form of alter personalities that
derive from repeated physical and sexual abuse. Alter personalities
are firmly grounded in the external world; each is capable of acknowledging the conditions of the world that surround it, although
that acknowledgment is specific to whatever alter happens to be
"out" and the kind of experience surrounding the alter's birth. Because of ongoing trauma usually beginning in infancy, the self has
been shattered. Grafted onto whatever being remains are numerous,
often separable and distinct personalities or part-personalities that
possess no knowledge of a continuing developmental line. What orients each alter is the specific abuse that gave rise to its existence; the
"self's" historical knowledge, therefore, is the knowledge of its own
terror.

No single, identifiable self in the multiple personality is capable
of integrating consciousness of the self's history with its movement
through psychodevelopmental stages of growth. The host personality often suffers from blackouts and memory lapses. It is as if the
self were made up of disconnected, noncommunicating images
whose existence in the world derived directly from terror and pain.
One moment a meek, withdrawn five-year-old appears; another a
dominating, hostile fifteen-year-old; another a violent, murderous
twenty-year-old, and so on. With this kind of multiplicity, whoever

enters the field of the multiple self finds a bewildering number of shifts in being and "becoming." This form of multiplicity lacks coherence and identity.

The origins of the multiple personalities I spoke with lay in the repeated violence of the father's incest and physical abuse and, in the case of satanic cults, the forced participation in sexual ritual and physical assault against persons and animals. Lacan's description of the incest taboo is relevant: "The primordial law is therefore that which in regulating marriage ties superimposes the kingdom of culture on that of nature abandoned to the law of copulation" (1968: 40). What distinguishes that primordial law is its injunction against incest, the basic proscription of the patriarchal order; the injunction defines the boundaries of culture, the limits of power. When the injunction is broken, the culture sinks to a precivil level—in the language of political theory, a prepolitical state, a Hobbesian "state of nature," a realm of pure unrestrained power. For over two years at Sheppard-Pratt I spoke with women for whom that law had been broken, whose lives were totally transformed and in some cases almost completely destroyed by the violation of the taboo against incest and the perverse imposition of power on the self.

The psychoanalytic feminist critique of "phallocracy" is an attack on the Law of the Father and the forms in which paternal law organizes society and culture (Brennan 1989). With women suffering multiple personality, the initial defining experience of self lies outside law; it occurs in a prepolitical space, without order, structure, or law—the space of pure power. The phallocracy the feminists argue against is predicated on the prohibition against incest; yet the father, incestuously violating his daughter, moves beyond law. His actions are a notorious violation, a criminal act breaking the taboo that defines basic structures of kinship. The abused child, left alone with a lawless phallocrat occupies a Hobbesian nature without the mediation of culture. I expand on this point in Chapter 4.

It is, however, possible to live emotionally in this state of nature, yet physically and cognitively reside in culture. The women who have suffered this very specific form of abuse (and the consequence of multiple personalities) live, work, marry, and lead lives in a culture ruled by patriarchal law.

To listen to these women's narratives is to witness extraordinary terror. Theirs is a grim universe in which the father ceases to be bound by any restraint other than his own desire. His daughter's body becomes a private fiefdom suffering the force of his will; the female body turns into a receptacle for an exercise of force moving, literally, beyond the confines of civil society. That force, and its presence, blocks the psychological connection of self with culture; it inhibits, if not prevents altogether, the creation of transitional objects (Winnicott 1982). In her terror, the child lives alone, isolated, without the protection and comfort of transitional spaces which facilitate the movement from precultural to cultural states. Instead of transitional objects, the child, repeatedly abused by her father, constructs alternate personalities that act as buffers between the force of reality and the survival of consciousness.

Nothing of the French feminists' celebration of the feminine exists in the multiple personality; it is as if any sense of the self's reality as a being apart from contextuality in male desire had disappeared through years of repeated abuse. Sexual identity invariably circulates around abuse, domination, and cruelty; marriages endure extraordinary abuse; sexual relationships act out violent themes. It is a tragic cycle, because the awareness of what the cycle means is closed to consciousness. Irigaray's sentiment of the unity of the feminine ("I love you: body shared, undivided. Neither you nor I severed. There is no need for blood shed between us. No need for a wound to remind us that blood exists" [1985a: 206]) lies outside these women's sense of who they are. Father and daughter know each other only as the disembodied pieces of a physical body; or, in Irigaray's terms: "The Other has no Other" (101). The thing the daughter has become, the function, possesses no soul: "Women don't have a soul: they serve as guarantee for man's" (97).

What is remarkable about both psychosis and multiple personality is how otherness defines the self through power: the power of delusion in the case of psychosis; the power of paternal abuse, rape, and terror in women with severe dissociative disorders.

Language and the Multiple Personality

For the multiple personality, otherness is born in the experience of terror; it has nothing to do with the Lacanian notion of the refraction of self in language, as reflected in Lacan's statement: "What I seek in the Word is the response of the other. . . . I identify myself in language, but only by losing myself in it like an object" (1968: 63). When the Other in the form of the father as terrorist invades the self's being, the personality responds not as a rational instrument but as a terrorized presence. To keep terror from literally imploding consciousness, the process of dissociation produces an alter personality to live through the force of the father's invasion. Tyranny, domination, and the unyielding will of authority forge the various manifestations of personality with their shifting frames of identity. Otherness emerges from a nondialectical matrix in which "being" is broken up (through nonverbal trauma) into discrete parts.

This self never in a fundamental psychological sense left the Imaginary, the precivil or prelinguistic position. This psychological environment is very much different from that in the Lacanian notion of an unconscious structured by the languages of culture. "In Lacanian theory," Stephen Frosh writes, "the subject is never separate from the social world, is always thoroughly permeated by it and liable to the distortions inculcated by the predominant ideology" (1987: 137). To be part of the symbolic is to exist within its languages and to have one's emotional world defined by those languages. Language, for Lacan, literally creates the unconscious. "The subject is in fact structured in and by ideology. . . . These ideological relations are institutionalised in culture and manifested in linguistic practice" (137). For the multiple personality, however, the reality of trauma shifts the locus of unconscious identification from the mediations of language to the terror of the father's presence. Identity or its knowledge, rather than being a linguistic practice, appears as a psychophysiological experience in which it is not language that structures the unconscious, but the presence of terror.

Because each self in a multiple personality possesses a different sense of the world, unknown to the so-called host personality, each alter constructs language describing realities specific to the alter's age of birth (e.g., JMG: "Why does Toby talk like she does?" E: "Because she's only seven years old; she will always be seven years old."). But this "language" or "text" composing pieces of the internal world exists in notoriously bad faith. Elaborate deceptions, complicated emotional patterns—these linguistic masks represent neither what is real or authentic, either in the person or in language.

They may be considered falsehoods constructed through dissociative mechanisms that protect consciousness from complete annihilation. What saved these women from becoming totally mad, schizophrenically fragmented, was the power of self-hypnosis (dissociation) and the capacity to forge alternative identities shielding, *through language*, the rape of the self and the experience of horror.

When the language of the alters is brought into the service of recollection, which establishes a common memory in the self—at that point language's defensive function transforms into an effort to speak the truth and thereby break down the compartmentalized structure of the multiple personalities and their "in-dwelling." Oftentimes that dialogue or cacophony occurs silently within the host's "mind," and the host or helper personality mediates argument and disagreement. Self-hypnosis, dissociative episodes—all combine to make the recognition of the condition extremely difficult in the absence of therapeutic mediation, a "place" where the "self," usually the host self, feels safe enough to endure the complications of intrapsychic communication among the alter personalities.

Each linguistic representation of an alter is an entity confined to a specific language that evolves around age-specific trauma. No alter possesses a "history" or an "evolution." Knowledge of who one is, then, has nothing to do with social discourses, with what Lacan calls a "chain of languages," because language encircles the self as compartmentalized defense.

For the multiple personality to have an authentic knowledge of her *self* would require facing the terror and the masks used to hide terror from consciousness. Even though the multiple personality lives in the social world, what motivates the self, its actions and representations, is a set of frozen, prelinguistic object relations framed by the desire of the father and the horror of his presence. Underlying each alter is an unstated, unspoken violation, an immense nonverbal darkness that holds the "reasons" for the multiple selves' existence.

Consciousness in the so-called normal person knows its orientation to experience through its power to remember, through language, the past. Further, from a Lacanian perspective, identity depends on prevailing discourses, their ideological function in culture and history, and their internalization by the subject (Ragland-Sullivan 1986). The language world of the multiple personality, however, is not connected historically nor is it constructed through the discourses of the symbolic or ideological order. No single language defines the *person-as-self*, nor is there a linear relationship among the personalities. Each alter, until the therapeutic deconstruction, is unaware of the existence of the others. From this perspective, the Lacanian notion of lack refers not to an emptiness in the self but to a terrorized core continuously creating personalities to protect or defend against a memory that literally froze the self, turned it to stone. Without a historic relation to experience, consciousness can never be sure of itself, because it is not at all clear which alter will be existentially "present."

For the multiple personality, memory, as the recovery of self, brings with it horror: memory is not a linguistic experience, because the languages of the alters provide critical defensive functions against memory. Multiplicity of identity, therefore, a multiplicity distinguished by the linguistic construction of alternate selves, becomes a plague.

Conclusion: The Anguish of the Fragmented Self

⸺ Lyotard's postmodernism "takes for granted that libidinal freefall will have a happy, rather than a tragic, result" (Ryan 1988: 563). If "libidinal freefall" means acting out different sexual identities or desires, that experience in the multiple personality may bring dislocation, alienation, and at times severe physical injury; to be sexually "multiple" in a multiple personality is not to have memory of action and events. Thus Judy simply has no recollection of the actions of Elizabeth, Toby, Mary, or Joe. The postmodern critique of order refuses to take into account the psychological need of the self for a frame of reference which possesses some object constancy. No human being can sustain "libidinal freefall" without a core self providing some kind of buffer against contingency. Indeed, the experience of multiple personalities testifies to the psychological consequences of finding oneself in a universe without limits, meaning, or fixed points of reference.

To witness a self in a state of freefall is a terrifying sight; to listen to a woman with multiple personalities describe the extent of her sexual abuse, and its origins in the violation of the infantile body, is to see a tragic freefall indeed. The woman's experience is similar to that in Irigaray's description: "Her own will is shattered so afraid is she of the master, so aware of her inner nothingness. And her work in the service of another, of that male Other, ensures the ineffectiveness of any desire that is specifically hers" (1985b: 225). That self endures an emotional state very much at odds with the postmodern celebration of boundlessness. Baudrillard, for example, writes, "All bound energies aim for their own demise." He believes the world therefore strikes the bound self, caught in fixed realities, tied to unyielding absolutes as *"catastrophic, and not in the least bit dialectical"* or fluid and freely moving without constraint (1988: 123). If one sees the world as dialectical or fluid, if the self chooses to move against bound and fixed frames of reference, Baudrillard argues, the only strategy, the only out, is to push experience "to the limit, where everything is naturally inverted and collapses" (a kind of joyous nihilism). It means thinking of playing at life as a kind of simulation or game, where the play of this game "must therefore be taken further than the system permits" (123). But in my clinical experience, where the self and its participatory universe are the central focus of analysis, the multiple personality does not enjoy a dialectics in the self; there is no pleasure in the falling away of fixed points of reference or in the experience and knowledge of break-up and fragmentation. Rather than creating pleasure, the collapse of a fixed self brings but the anguish of multiple selves, existing in relation to one another as static, unmoving, and transfixed presences.

It is quite an assumption in postmodern philosophy that a self can disintegrate or break into discrete pieces without terrible consequences; possibly some selves can endure this kind of nihilism, this unattached, disconnected sense of what reality is and what relationships imply. But it is a dangerous psychological game, nonetheless, this "death" playing "against death" (123).

Multiple personalities and schizophrenics who live within the experiential nexus of Baudrillard's "hyperlogic of destruction and death" need not limitlessness or nihilism (the environment of delusion; Glass 1985) but the opposite, a world of meaning and definable space and time which gives to the self a sense of its own historical position in the world. Self-coherence and playful identity are in a clinical sense not the products of nihilistic abandonment but derive from efforts to frame experience in meaning, to discover an ontological position that might repair whatever psychological damage the self has suffered. "Being," then, for the multiple personality refers not to blasting away at the limits of the self but to finding those limits and moving away from boundless expanse, the anarchic free-fall of fragmented identities and endless becoming.

It might be argued, "How can you use the experience of this very special population to make critical judgments about a philosophical position?"—fair enough. But the postmodernists, especially such cutting-edge theorists as Baudrillard and Lyotard, are saying more than that the self should be plural in its interests, moods, and expressions; theirs is not simply another statement of an existential pluralism, a "liberalism" advocating plural attitudes, ways of life, or critical judgments. If the philosophy of postmodernism is to be more than a restatement of liberal pragmatism, its theory of multiple identity suggests a dangerous theory of disconnection in the self, a kind of psychological nihilism. Disconnected selves that have lost any will or meaning, who live in the midst of a free-floating nothingness, at least clinically suffer an extraordinary alienation—not only the alienation of discrete, and separable, personalities in multiple personality disorder, but the fragmentation characteristic of the schizophrenic: the imploded self, without being or connection to any consensual histories. Deleuze and Guattari's use of the schizophrenic's experience as a kind of revolutionary model misses entirely the terrible psychological costs of a fragmented existence: a severing of the self's connection to any known and recognizable consensual reality and existence in a delusional space in which otherness appears in the nihilistic wanderings of delusional action.

A related argument against my position might be phrased: "If multiple personality disorder is a response to catastrophe—specifically paternal sexual abuse—rather than a cause of it, then without that catastrophe the consequence would look and feel very different." I would reply that multiplicity of identity, no matter what its cause, becomes, in its form as lived existence, a source of extraordinary torment and pain, whether it be the multiplicity of the multiple personality or the multiplicity of the fragmented schizophrenic. In its context as lived reality, multiplicity of self is not cause for celebration or joy. What is important here is the effect, the existence of multiplicity. To fracture an identity, to make multiple identities, requires a process of psychological deconstruction: consciousness would either have to be a consummate actor (an "as if" personality), a chameleon that is itself a pathological condition, or a multiple personality; schizophrenia would involve fragmented part-selves without any recognizable coherence. The deconstruction or, better, destruction, of self is not a pleasing sight in persons who have actually experienced the reality of identities without boundary or context in historical development.

If postmodernism is a philosophy dealing only on the level of texts and with the play of ideas, then the theory of multiplicity takes on an aesthetic significance, to be used as a critical and interpretive instrument. My central theoretical point is that multiple identities or personalities derive not from a pleasurable decentering (the activity of textual analysis, an intellectual process) but from an intolerable, invasive, and patriarchal source or center that annihilates in and on the body any potential or possibility for pleasure.

One may choose multiple tastes and interests; one may decide for whatever reason to be different or eccentric or to hold values that counter established assumptions and preferences. One does not choose, however, to possess a multiple or fragmented identity: those effects, either in multiple personality disorder or schizophrenia, are the products of a social and psychological violence that rips apart being, terrorizes the self, and brutalizes the body. The multiplicity of identity or personality is a commentary on some of the most pathological aspects of a deranged modernity that idealizes paternal authority and the violent imposition of power.

4   PHALLOCRATIC CULTURE
AND REVERSION TO THE
STATE OF NATURE

Much that is of interest in recent French feminist theory embodies a reaction to Lacanian psychoanalysis (Frosh 1987; Weedon 1987). These critics take issue with Lacan's association of patriarchal authority and the rule of the phallus with the symbolic order and the order of language and culture (Feldstein and Roof 1989). For the psychoanalytic feminists, that association and its implicit assumptions about power, reason, and structure constitute the chief aim of their attack (Flax 1987).

The Phallocrat

Irigaray's postmodern/psychoanalytic/feminist perspective is important in situating the experience of the multiple personality within a theoretical discourse considerably different from the psychiatric technicalism that dominates the professional literature on multiple personality.

For example, she argues, with Lacan, that language, as the "signifier" of the rational, evolves from a cultural matrix of power, domination, order, and regularity. But she believes that language suffers from its domination by the symbolic order that itself represents the signs of male authority and power, what Irigaray calls "phallocentrism." She compares the language of domination with the laws of solid mechanics and physics and argues for a feminine linguistics likened to a theory of fluid mechanics. "Solid mechanics and rationality have maintained a relationship of very long standing, one against which fluids have never stopped arguing" (1985a: 113). What she finds necessary is a language that flows, a language that like "fluid . . . is, by nature, unstable. . . . How can it be defined with respect to the properties, also, of fluids? Milk, luminous flow, acoustic waves" (112–13). Woman—as she appears in the *language* of flow, interruption, discontinuity, suppleness—questions the domination of rational discourse and its linguistic structures. "Woman never speaks the same way. What she emits is flowing, fluctuating. *Blurring.*" Male-rational discourse tries to "congeal[s], freeze[s]" language through "its categories until it paralyzes the voice in its flow" (112).[1] The phallocrat murders the flow of the female voice; he becomes its destroyer—the phallocrat freezes expression.

My experience with the clinical reality of multiple personality reflects this perspective. The isolated phallocrat marauds the psychological state of nature. When he repudiates his own law, the cultural proscription against incest, the power of his autocratic desire displaces the power *and* legislative context of male reason (the incest taboo as the social contract). It is a shift in venue: the phallocrat who rules by law in the world of culture is now totally unconstrained, even by legislative reason, in the isolated nature of his ferocious desire; he finds himself willingly denying cultural reality (Lacan's symbolic) for his private excursion into sexual violence. In this peculiar, depraved state of nature, the father annihilates his daughter's presence; he denies the possibility of reciprocity and affection; he attacks the limit-creating potential of culture through its moral frameworks; and he thoroughly repudiates the "commodious" life, to borrow a phrase from Thomas Hobbes.

---

[1]Irigaray's notion of fluidity and multiplicity is intensely metaphoric and symbolic. While "fluidity" as a model for a life free of existential constraint might be "healthy" for a resilient ego, it could be disastrous for the self prone to regression or splitting. Does it make sense, for example, for a person with highly volatile "borderline" qualities to be on a quest for fluidity? It may be that fluidity is precisely the psychological symptom that needs to be treated. Although I am sympathetic to Irigaray's position, and although I believe Kristeva to be sensitive to the issue of multiplicity (and coherence) in a clinical context, these concepts, precisely because of their metaphoric properties, fail to provide the self with a workable "ground."

For the multiple personality, what characterize this psychological state of nature are rigid languages whose solidity is not a celebration of existence but a desperate defense against the horror of utter annihilation. To listen to a five-year-old Katy or seven-year-old Laura or twelve-year-old Eddy describe what Daddy "did" is to witness a transgression of taboo that transforms discourse into force. It is to see in language a preoedipal world distinguished by dread and the effects of an exploded self coming together in what appear to be discrete wholes but which are in reality dissected parts of age-specific trauma.

The multiple personality creates a world out of nothingness; but the story she tells is a narrative commenting on the terror of being; the various personas circulate like eviscerated selves, each of whom owes its existence to the murderous indifference of the father's desire. These personalities emerge out of the experience of psychological annihilation and entombment, and the multiplicity of the multiple personality derives from the force of the phallocrat who himself has left the civil community.

When the father's desire breaks down the law, it destroys patriarchal order, the governing prerogatives of clan-based regulation, the binding effect of kinship ties, and the symbolic relations governing community. The father's contempt for the incest taboo throws the father-daughter dyad into an emotional space frozen in time—a state that precedes the unitary politics of the phallocracy. The condition suggests a serious weakness in the capacity of patriarchal law to maintain the prohibition on incest and therefore to protect the culture and its women from the depredations of unrestrained force.

The violation of the incest taboo demonstrates a contempt for the basic foundation of a politics that guarantees, at least sexually, the integrity of the civil compact. Arrogance, sexual depravity, and the disrespect for "being" and law create an anarchy in the family in which the child's personality in order to survive must kill itself over and over again. The effects of that repeated killing appear in the masks of the many different personalities occupying one body.

I emphasize: certainly, sexual abuse constitutes a perversion of the law of patriarchy, which is, as I see it, what Irigaray, Jane Gallop, Clément, and others are arguing. But whether the violent debasement and invasion of the female infant and child can be considered to be part of the totemic law that binds the social structure of paternal power is another issue altogether. From what I heard from women with multiple personalities, it was not so much the "law" of male prerogative or power which abused and hurt them but a beast-like presence in the world beyond any law or constraint, beyond the law of the family, the law of the state, the "laws" of common decency. The Law of the Father does not protect or condone the kind of depravity which creates multiple personality disorder. One of the central injunctions behind the incest taboo and preservation of the family is that sexual desire find exogamous "sites" for its satisfaction.

Freud, too, argued that not only did the incest taboo compose a law whose purpose was to guarantee the prerogative of male power, but its existence also served to protect the family, particularly the women of the family, from sexual abuse or appropriation by phallocentric desire, whether it be the will of the father or the impulses of the sons and brothers. It is important here to distinguish between unrestrained "will" (the phallocrat transgressing the limits of his daughter's body) and paternal "law," or forms of power designed by a male-dominant civilization to assure order, stability, and continuity, particularly in regards to property. Why would patriarchy want to debase its central propertied "commodity," what Irigaray and Gallop see as the exchange of women? It is for this reason that forms of patriarchal law should be distinguished from the debasement of law produced by the unrestrained paternal "will" sexually violating the daughter's body.[2]

<hr />

[2]For an interesting discussion of the nature of exchange and its relation to the status of women as possessing exchange-value, see Pateman 1988. She writes: "The momentous step from nature to culture, [Lévi-Strauss] maintains, comes about through the institution of the prohibition against incest, or the law of exogamy. This law has a unique status; it is a social rule which, like the laws of nature, is universal. The prohibition of incest marks the great dividing-line between nature and culture, or civilization. The law is the means through which nature is transcended. Once exogamy is the rule, men must find wives from outside their own social group (family). . . . Lévi-Strauss sees marriage as the archetype of exchange. . . . Marriage, or the orderly exchange of women, which gives equal sexual access to all men, is the original exchange that constitutes culture or civilization. Once culture is created, women cease to be mere 'natural stimulants' and become signs of social value. . . . When a woman becomes a 'wife,' her husband gains rights of sexual access to her body (once called 'conjugal rights' in legal language) and to her labour as a housewife" (110, 111, 115). The phallocrat so degrades his daughter as to deplete her of social exchange value. Incest throws not only the relation between male and female, but the very presence of the

The Unitary Self and Phallocracy

A recurrent theme of the French feminists is the critique of unicity, the unitary self, seen as the self of male logic, the disciplines of domination (psychiatry, law, the social and physical sciences, and so on). Rationality signifies the Law of the Father. But, I would argue, it is not necessarily the case that the wish or desire for a sense of self-coherence or unity means a desire for domination, the submission of consciousness to phallocratic logic. It is certainly not always the case with the multiple personality. What is peculiar about multiple personalities is that the source of domination, the condition of nonfreedom in the self, lies not only in the arrogance of phallocratic power but also in the brutality and egoism of often tormenting multiple identities.

In the philosophical critique of unicity and its origins in Cartesian reason which runs through Irigaray's writings, the concept of the *one*, a patriarchal institution, is seen as dangerous, a threat to female discontinuity and "flow." But from a clinical point of view, it would be difficult to argue that the goal of therapy for the multiple personality should not focus on an internal resolution in which the boundaries between alters break down and a stable, central self is created.

For Gallop and Irigaray, the "rule of the Phallus is the reign of the *One*, of Unicity" (Gallop 1982a: 66; and see Irigaray 1985a). Patriarchal law denotes a "sublimated male homosexuality structuring all our institutions: pedagogy, marriage, commerce, even Freud's theory of so-called heterosexuality." The power of rational unitary *male* logic creates "structures [that] necessarily exclude women, but are unquestioned because sublimated . . ." (64). Unicity, as a theory of domination, a product of male reason and Cartesian rationality, stands behind the patriarchal injunctions that appear as law in societies governed by male prerogative. Such "reason" Irigaray sees as the product of the "phallocratic order . . . masculine parameters" (1985a: 81, 155) and derives, according to Gallop from the "male ho-

---

female body, back into a state of nature, where only force governs the abuse and destruction of value.

mosexual economy" (1982a: 74). Patriarchal law "is supposed to be just—that is, impartial, indifferent, free from desire" (75), but the extreme sexual abuse suffered by the multiple personality severs the relation between self and law; the self never attains a level of psychological development which would assure at least a fixed sense of sexual identity and a narcissism located within a single self framed by a given history. For her, to exist as a "she" is to live as a depleted thing masked by the counterdiscourses of multiple identity.

It makes little sense to speak of a linear identity, a unitary self, for a woman whose presence in the world, both existentially and in terms of memory, depends on a number of different personalities. Moving through phases of development would be inconsistent, because each self is born at a fixed point in time. No single self, then, in the multiple personality may be said to move through, for example, in Margaret Mahler's terms, symbiosis, attachment, separation, and individuation (Mahler et al. 1975). The three-year-old remains three; the seven-year-old, seven, even when each appear years later as a powerful alter. In this melange of static, compartmentalized selves, "normal" psychological development or normal narcissism as a reliable foundation for a stable identity becomes extraordinarily problematic.

Incest and the Political Economy

In *Speculum of the Other Woman*, Irigaray writes, "*The father . . . legislates to defend himself from*" the desire to seduce his daughter (1982b: 76, Irigaray's italics). Law protects the male as ruler from the intensity and danger of his incestuous desire. Without the prohibition of law, and without its sanctions, the father becomes a threat not only to the women of the culture but also to his sons and brothers. "The father's law is a counterphobic mechanism. He must protect himself from his desire for the daughter. His desire for the feminine threatens his narcissistic overvaluation of his penis" (Gallop 1982a: 76). Crossing the boundary into incest, I would suggest, destroys that protection; the father or patriarchy's law fails, and the daughter becomes the sacrifice, the object of desire and its tragic victim. It is her *body* that inscribes the narrative of victimization.

Gallop and Irigaray see the prohibition of incest in political society as an economic issue. The prohibition is functional to male power in the sense that it enables the father to place a value on his daughter in relation to the surrounding culture. That value appears as an exchange relation and situates male desire within a matrix of political economy. Possessing the daughter sexually moves against the main lines of economic interest; it violates the compact and removes the daughter's self and body as a marketable commodity. The father, rather than seeing his daughter as an extension of his own family heritage in a civil world (exogamy), sees her as his own private preserve. She becomes a thing gratifying the hidden force of his desire, a "place" marked by the savagery of need, but not a valued commodity (intended for an open market) understood as an extension of her father's economic position. Gallop explains: "If the father were to desire his daughter, he could no longer exchange her, no longer possess her in the economy by which true, masterful possession is the right to exchange. If you cannot give something up for something of like value, if you consider it nonsubstitutable, then you do not possess it any more than it possesses you. So the father must not desire the daughter for that threatens to remove him from the homosexual commerce in which women are exchanged between men, in the service of power relations and community for the men" (1982a: 76). Thus the prohibition on incest not only performs a powerful psychological function in maintaining the cultural matrix and its symbolic forms, it also creates a space wherein women can be exchanged for marketable value. The prohibition gives to women value within law. Phallocracy as the "name" for this legal order assures preservation but for a price. Irigaray describes the relation: "In our social order, women are 'products' used and exchanged by men. Their status is that of merchandise, 'commodities.' How can such objects of use and transaction claim the right to speak and to participate in exchange in general? Commodities, as we all know, do not take themselves to market on their own. . . . So women have to remain an 'infrastructure' unrecognized as such by our society and our culture. The use, consumption and circulation of their sexualized bodies underwrite the organization and the reproduction of the social order, in which they have never taken part as 'subjects' " (1985a: 84).

For the incestuously abusive father, his daughter is a property that has a specific use-value in relation to desire. Desire, not markets or economic exchange, defines the body-as-property: "the *organization and monopolization of private property to the benefit of the head of the family*" (Irigaray 1985a: 83). Repeated sexual abuse, the use of the daughter in cult rituals, the giving of the child sexually to friends in payment of debts (a synthesis of the body as "property-in-desire" and "property-as-exchange value")—all these actions described to me by patients carry the concept of the body-as-private property of the father to perverse extremes.

The phallocrat who stalks the state of nature, who desires his daughter and therefore removes from her any value in relation to the rest of the culture, has no interest in the civil world. This father, a renegade, defines himself as a criminal presence within a patriarchy founded on the law regulating sexuality within the family and attacks the very foundations of civil and moral order. Incestuous abuse removes the daughter's value from the exchange relations of political economy and threatens the daughter's potential for reproduction within kinship systems.

Sexuality and the Multiple Personality

This continuing use of the body of the self as the father's exclusive "desiring machine" (to borrow a phrase from Deleuze and Guattari 1977) places the daughter not only beyond the protection of the law but even beyond the seductive desire of fantasized attachments. The result is seen in the despair of women who confess a hopelessness over even the possibility of life itself, who hate what they are and feel an enormous frustration over ever being "whole" or "one" or "unitary." For such women, the father never possessed a fantasized oedipal function; nor did his presence contribute to lines of desire that developed the female self's autonomy, capacity for affection, and externalized object attachments. Instead, he became torturer, not to be distinguished from any torturer whose objective lies in defiling the body and spirit.

For the multiple personality, what it means to be female appears only in the context defined by each specific alter. That meaning always involves violence and degradation. Femaleness possesses nothing of Irigaray's notion of female erotogenicity: "In fact, a woman's erogenous zones are not the clitoris or the vagina, but the clitoris and the vagina, and the lips, and the vulva, and the mouth of the uterus, and the uterus itself and the breasts" (1985a: 63–64). In the context of the multiple personality's sexual experience, these "zones" become sites for the purpose of terror. And although Irigaray celebrates the "multiplicity of genital erogenous zones . . . in female sexuality" (64), that multiplicity and its *presence* for women with several different identities turns into torment and confusion.

The oedipal yearnings of the little girl also disintegrate under the force of the reality of abuse. Irigaray's Kleinian understanding of fantasy as a description of the origins of a girl's sexuality has no meaning for these victims. She writes, in a reading that might be clinically relevant for women with relatively "normal" psychological and sexual development: "Oedipal precocity no doubt has its dangers. The father's penis is capable of satisfying the little girl's desires, but it can also, and at the same time, destroy. It is 'good' and 'bad,' life-giving and death-dealing, itself caught up in the implacable ambivalence between love and hate, in the duality of the life and death instincts. In addition, the first attraction for the father's penis has the father as its aim, insofar as his organ has already been introjected by the mother. Thus, the girl would take possession of the paternal penis, and potentially of the children, that are contained in the mother's body" (54).

The abused daughter possesses no psychological avenues enabling her to create a seductive fantasy about the relationship; she has no internal space from which to construct out of the father's presence a fantasized object of love and affection. He lives in her mind as a stark reality, without any modulation or softening by the power of internal object representations. The absolute perversion of human intentionality dominates their relationship. There is nothing here of the Freudian "wish." For this little girl, desire appears not as the sexual wish for love but as the disintegrating morbidity of death, the wish for nonbeing. There is no attraction, no life instinct, just fear of pain. What is "desired" is not the father's penis but a liberation, a nirvana of spirit and body, a radical escape from the very physicalness of the father's body and his presence as an instrument of violence. The alter personalities serve as avenues of escape. The phallocrat perverts fantasy; the little girl does not "desire" the penis; nor does she wish to give her daddy babies. Father's penis *is* the source of her pain; *she* is the baby being violated. The father as person and phallocrat produces identities framed in the affect of "badness." Desire in the multiple personality defines itself not through fantasy and the erotic stimulation of fantasized attachments but through the harshness of a reality which possesses nothing of the erotic.

The *fantasy* component of the multiple personality, then, appears not in the realm of desire but in the realm of escape and nonbeing. Thus, within the imaginary world of the multiple self, there will inevitably be a "helper" personality who provides refuge (e.g., "the lady who takes me to the forest" or alters who create an amnesia), while the body and its accompanying alter are "left" behind to experience the rape.

Even masochistic fantasies become radically transformed when understood through the reality of the multiple personality. For example, Irigaray comments on fantasy "in which the little girl's incestuous desires would find both regressive masochistic satisfaction and punishment . . . This fantasy might also be interpreted as follows: my father is beating me in the guise of the boy I wish I were; or else: I am being beaten because I am a girl, that is, inferior, sexually speaking; or, in other words: what is being beaten is my clitoris, that very small, too small male organ, that little boy who refuses to grow up" (1985a: 45). That fantasy, however, would have no place in the world of the multiple personality: force drives out oedipal imagination or unconscious wish. The facts of being beaten and hurt have nothing to do with fantasy or with an effort to move unconsciously closer to what is perceived as the father's wish. Masochism in the multiple personality possesses reasons and explanations rooted in reality, in life experience itself, not in fantasized projections. Even though the self-representation of "badness" pervades the multiple personality's being, her fear of the world derives not from internal projections (in, for example, the Kleinian sense: Alford 1989) but from the extremity of her father's desire and its embodiment in the brutality of rape.

The origins of masochistic identification in the multiple personality, the sense of self-hatred and self-disgust, indicate not an idealization of the father in the form of desire but the derailment of desire, the unconscious repudiation of oedipal wishes, the skidding away of the self from the control of the law, and descent to an anarchic natural condition in which desire takes as its object whatever lies in its field.

Desire and the Multiple Personality

Must the "multiplicity of female desire and female language be understood as shards, scattered remnants of a violated sexuality? A sexuality denied?" Irigaray asks. And while she says that "the question has no simple answer" (1985a: 30), it certainly has a clear answer for women repeatedly raped from childhood by their fathers. The father here excludes the presence of the maternal: mothers are notoriously absent in the lives of these women; they do not offer safety or nurturance. The father denies to his daughter any imaginary world separate and apart from the rape as lived experience and the facticity of alter personalities. Or, in Irigaray's terms: "The exclusion of a female imaginary certainly puts woman in the position of experiencing herself only fragmentarily, in the little-structured margins of a dominant ideology, as waste, or excess" (for the multiple personality, the father's "waste or excess"). She continues, "The role of 'femininity' [what is femininity in a woman with several different personalities, some of whom may be male?] is prescribed by this masculine specula(riza)tion and corresponds scarcely at all to woman's desire." Finally, desire that is specifically woman's finds itself excluded from the range of masculine images and fantasies; it "may be recovered only in secret, in hiding, with anxiety and guilt" (30).

Women, Irigaray writes, find "pleasure almost anywhere. . . . [T]he geography of [women's] pleasure is far more diversified [than is males'], more multiple in its difference, more complex, more subtle, than is commonly imagined—in an imaginary rather too narrowly focused on sameness" (28). That is certainly true for women not plagued with the consequences of persistent childhood rape, but for the infant and child whose bodies become the private fiefdom of their father's desire, whatever is multiple in the self's "being" as identity is symptomatic—not a sign of the possibility in the feminine or the maternal relation, but a sign of the domination of the father, his force and will.

For the multiple personality, to recover desire is to break down the compartmentalized secrecy of the self. It is to become free of the legacy and tragedy of the body's rape through the consolidation of an identity from the many selves that occupy the same body. That consolidation is a process, a slow merging of the different affects that seem to define each alter, in addition to a synthesis of meaning and history which arises from the common experience of all the recognizable alters. It is to leave trauma as lived memory, memory as an existential present ("abreaction"), and to enter the symbolic order in which experience is subject to the distancing capacities of a language capable of remembering a history.

5 MOLLY'S ABSENCE OF SELF AND THE POSTMODERN CRITIQUE

Postmodernists argue for a world without meaning, for randomness, for decentering. Before I present Molly's multiple personality, I look at some psychological implications of the postmodernist position, specifically at such notions as uncertainty, fragmentation, multiplicity, and identity as context for her discussion. I am particularly concerned with what is involved in living with multiple identities, with the impact of multiplicity on self-knowledge. I conclude with some of Baudrillard's observations on evil and surrealism which directly address Molly's terrifying state and which, in this regard, may be helpful in describing and understanding the despair of the multiple personality's experience.

Postmodern philosophy conceptualizes the self as a series of falsehoods, strung together by the endlessly repeating productions of what Baudrillard calls "simulation." The self turns into a massive simulacrum, a series of fragments representing only the force of disembodied power and the repetitive dullness of imitation. Any view of human experience or desire which posits an underlying essence or structure is a massive illusion, playing to the self's need for security in a radically uncertain world.

Postmodernism, in Baudrillard's reading, inaugurates a "second revolution, that of the twentieth century, of post-modernity, which is the immense process of the destruction of meaning, equal to the earlier destruction of appearances. Whoever lives by meaning dies by meaning" (1984b: 38–39). It is a particularly grim view of the human capacity for value, as Douglas Kellner describes it: "Meaning requires depth, a hidden dimension, an unseen substratum; in postmodern society, however, everything is visible, explicit, transparent, obscene. The postmodern scene exhibits signs of dead meaning, dissection and transparency, excremental culture, frozen forms mutating into new combinations and permutations of the same" (1988: 246). Meaning remains a dead relic of modernist ideologies and faiths.

If women with multiple personalities and schizophrenics with fragmented, disconnected identities suggest the fate of imploded selves, selves without meaning, context, history, or form, then the experience of these persons might indicate the dangers of what Baudrillard refers to as a game, "playing with the pieces" of "what is left" after fragmentation (1984a: 24–25). But what are these "pieces" when understood in the context of the self?

For the multiple personality, or the schizophrenic, living with the fragments is not a game but a terrifying journey through the lived experience of fragmentation and death. And the horror of living in a world without boundaries and meaning suggests a human cost simply not acknowledged in the nihilism of postmodernist expression. What women with multiple personalities teach is the logic of multiplicity, where it goes, its consequences, and the entropy that threatens the self in a nihilist universe.

The French feminists, however, warn against the embracing of nothingness; their argument for rethinking and reconstructing *feminine* identity, particularly in their emphasis on discourse and writing, places their theory outside of the nihilist and often gender-blind tendencies of postmodern philosophy. This linking of freedom from phallocentric authority and the creation of feminine identity Clément puts in a striking way: "As long as the sorceress [a metaphor of the unconstrained feminine self] is still free, at the sabbat, in the forest, she is a sensitivity that is completely exposed—all open skin, natural, animal, odorous, and deliciously dirty. When she is caught [that is, when she finds herself subject to phallocratic authority], when the scene of the inquisition is formed around her, in the same way the medical scene later forms around the hysteric, she withdraws into herself, she cries, she has numb spots, she vomits. She has become hysterical [a victim of social discourses and practices enforced by paternal law]" (Cixous and Clément 1986: 39). For Clément, the process of attaining a sense of feminine identity brings with it pain; witness, she argues, the hysteric's frightening efforts to rid herself of the "otherness" of an oedipal *his*tory: "The father is the Law; the austerity of the Symbolic, the privileged force of the order, comes from the looming, immemorial figure of the prehistoric father. This father is overpossessive: the perverse Law. Thou shalt love none other than me. The hysterics' narratives put into question the social structure in its family roots, in the thread of generations each succeeding the other" (45).

It is, however, exactly what the postmodernists criticize, the search for meaning, which lifts women with multiple personalities from their misery and self-destructiveness, from the illusory non-being of multiplicity, and situates them in a human dialectic, a therapeutic reconstruction, that holds the promise of coherence, structure, and continuity of historical remembrance. I am not arguing that multiple personalities should be understood as proof or disproof of any philosophical theory: only that the extremity of this condition, the experiential intensity of living within massive simulations (alter personalities simulating reality by literally re-presenting it), demonstrates how terrifying it is to live out this most "postmodernist" form of knowledge, and how dangerous it can be to "live" in a meaningless world or *gestalt* without certainty, anchors, or epistemological structure. To "play" at this way of life is to court enormous psychological danger.

Nor do I maintain that intellectually playing with multiplicity brings with it the horrors of multiple personality; certainly playing or playfulness with words, ideas, images, and concepts appears in the literary criticism and textual analysis of many postmodernists, including philosophers, novelists, and filmmakers. Playing at aesthetics or the artistry of postmodern "creativity" is not at issue. The primary question I address in this book is: What does it mean to live, on a day-to-day basis, with a fragmented, multiple self?

Cohesion, system, certainty, unity, even continuity, Baudrillard argues, are illusions supported and enforced by ideology and the morbid remains of modernist theorists of power and interpretation. He writes, "An example of this eccentricity of things, of this drift into excrescence, is the irruption of randomness, indeterminacy and relativity within our system." Dominant social ideologies, tied to dependent explanations, prolong the illusion of linear certainty, "these values of reference, function, finality and causality" (1988: 188).

Postmodernist analyses of mass society, the fatuousness of consumerism, the quiet terror of everyday life, raise important points. I would submit, however, there are good reasons to celebrate finality and causality and not indeterminacy—compelling psychological reasons. To reject indeterminacy does not mean that one has to ignore social contradiction or the deleterious effects of consumer society and the fetishism of consumption. In mental patients with severe disorders, the lack of certainty or object constancy may lead to a deadly sense of disintegration; in this respect, *not* to resist indeterminacy fosters, even encourages, forms of psychological fragmentation, with possibly disastrous effects on the self's interior life. It is this effect of what Baudrillard calls the "hyperreal" on the interior of the self, an implosive *fragmentation*, which postmodernist philosophy puts aside with flippant statements about the joy of "irony."

Postmodernism does offer useful perspectives on pleasurable decentering (bliss, or what Barthes calls *"jouissance"*). Certainly the call for openness to new forms of experience, an appreciation of the novel, different, and eccentric, a distrust for moribund and oppressive ideologies, a rejection of traditional authorities, and a sensitivity to the destructiveness of modernity are useful insights or pleasures. But that call is not exactly what the embracing of nihilism and the celebration of fragmentation is all about. Nor is it clear that the only route to these aims lies through postmodernist analysis; why not through critical theory or a rights-centered theory of liberalism, for example? Postmodernism calls for multiple selves, without taking into account the psychological effects of literally living with multiple (discrete) selves within the same body. That is an entirely different issue from the metatheoretical social criticism that distinguishes such philosophers as Baudrillard, Lyotard, Irigaray, and to a lesser extent Derrida and Rorty. The rejection of epistemology, fixed identities, and theories of being, coupled with the call for the proliferation of multiple selves, involves more than a dalliance with style, taste, or irony. It is in fact a radical rejection of the concept of identity, as well as of the psychoanalytic tradition's emphasis, including

that of the French psychoanalytic feminists, on the historical importance of sexuality and desire in the construction of self-knowledge.

The insistence on structure and causality, Baudrillard argues, enhances the power of capital and capitalism. But is structure only a
function of the organization of economic power? Is all causality only
ideologically defined? Or might structure be considered a property
of being itself, therefore a "property" the self desperately needs to
survive? The ideological posturing of modernism, masquerading as
truth, should, as an analytical matter, be separated from considerations regarding psychological structure. To reject "truth" in this
sense does not imply that one has to reject identity understood as
structural integrity. One can be sympathetic to the postmodernist
criticism of truth and the role illusion plays in social life without
rejecting conceptions of psychological reality and structure. The
structureless self is pathetic, as lost, alienated, and without meaning
as the empty souls of the hyperreal world.

It is irresponsible, dangerously seductive, to respond to a social
world of disintegration and fragmentation with an approach to self
that celebrates entropy. Baudrillard takes this celebration to extremes: "We will not seek change, nor oppose the fixed and the
mobile; we will seek what is more mobile than the mobile: metamorphosis" (1988: 185). Quite a project! Yet this is precisely what
the multiple personality wants to escape: metamorphosis, as a continuing and haunting indeterminacy of being. Look at some of the
dangers in unrestrained "metamorphosis": Kafka's Gregor Samsa
changed into a form beyond its recognition; the layering of self upon
self in women with multiple personalities, an existence so muddled
by multiplicity that even the host self mutters in despair, "Whenever
will I know myself?" Yet Baudrillard, who exemplifies this postmodernist position, refuses his audience any rescue: postmodernity
demands the self give up its need for security and structure. "Having been plunged into an in-ordinate uncertainty by randomness,
we [modern society] have responded by an excess of causality and
teleology" (1988: 189). But is the problem with finding causality?

Persons affected by randomness, driven crazy by it, require some
sense of meaning, a *telos* that allows consciousness to discover a
continuity, a history. To live without a history is to live in a placeless
universe; the self without a sense of place, a history to call its own,

an enclosure in community, a cohesive sense of its own internality: these kinds of "selves" wander silently in the corridors of mental hospitals. Placelessness, whether psychological or physical, breeds despair; it leads to insanity.

Molly: The Voices of Multiplicity

Molly's narrative has a tragic dimension, but tragedy without a public, an audience; the pain lies silently within the self, beyond the protection of law and civil society, spread out over a range of personas each holding experiences of terror and isolation.

Coldness and indifference experienced at the hands of abusive parental authority, usually the father, is a persistent theme in the narratives of women with multiple personality, as I have noted. Molly's condition is a painful example.

The more I listened to Molly,[1] the more curious I became as to how to make sense of Molly's world. Was hers an isolated case of a perverted and sick father or an extreme manifestation of a war on women, a disdain for their bodies and their beings, an absolute denial of personhood to the feminine (Irigaray's phallocentric culture acting out its most twisted logic), which included the feminine as a private preserve for the father, whose pleasure lay only in the imposition of power?

The tyrant's style is to annihilate; something similar happens to the multiple personality torn apart by a form of power that occupies her body, abuses her consciousness and body as a matter of a God-taken right to impose on her the terms of his desire. What does such a "god" or phallocrat create?

"He started touching me at two; at four we had sexual intercourse." That observation began our dialogue.

Molly called her alters "little people," and their presence was determined by sexual violence and gratuitous acts of physical and emotional cruelty. For example, Molly had to watch pigs slaughtered; she held their legs, as intestines and guts spilled out; she stood

---

[1]Molly (not her real name) is a forty-two-year-old, divorced mother of a teenage daughter. She grew up in a rural setting in the Midwest; she married when she was twenty. Until her hospitalization, she held an administrative position with a large multinational company with headquarters in the town near where she was born.

guard on hot summer days over the pigs' severed heads, covered with swarms of huge horse flies. Yet, although the body of the person standing guard was Molly, an alter appeared to experience the event.

The alters possessed different names at different ages: Little Girl (2–4), Girl (4–6), Mute (6), Elizabeth (10–11), Abbie, Abigail (13), Lizzie (14), Maggie (19), Jane (23), Black (no specific age), and Clear (rescuer or helper personality without any determinate age). These were only a few of the many personalities, fragments, and part selves inside Molly. But these personalities made themselves known to me. Each performed a different function; each was born at a specific age; each was a reaction to a specific traumatic event; and each remained within the "personality" as a self-contained, discrete entity, appearing with regular although unpredictable frequency.

⎯The age at which alters were born indicates when significant trauma occurred. Alters may have appeared earlier, but Molly was not then aware of their presence. Some alters appeared and then disappeared, remaining latent for several years. For example, Lizzie first emerged at age fourteen when she tried to kill Russell, Molly's father. Lizzie picked up the knife and screamed, "I'll get you for this; you deserve to die; you're scum for everything you've done to me and [her brothers and sisters]." She stabbed him and rubbed his blood in his face. (According to Elizabeth, Lizzie had been "out" during many earlier rapes. The layering of personalities may complicate identifying specific birth dates.)

Russell's sexual abuse followed Molly throughout her childhood and early adolescence. From time to time, he dragged Molly into bed with her mother. But her mother either ignored what went on or (she claimed) was sleeping. Molly remembers her mother as constantly strung out on tranquilizers; her mother never interfered with Russell's abuse. Molly's father died in his early fifties; he strangled on his own vomit after unusually heavy drinking.

Elizabeth wrote the following letter to God early on in her hospitalization:

God I am scared, It is night. During the day it is easy to be brave but at night it is hard. He is downstairs watching T.V. Maybe he will fall asleep and not come up here. I'm tired, wait, T.V. went off. I am in trouble now. He is on the steps, God forgive me. God forgive me. 'Now I lay me down to sleep' . . . forgive me please. O thanks. He went into the kitchen. Maybe he will get drunk and sleep in there. . . . He is coming. I cannot take this anymore. 'If I die before I wake.' Please let me die to end this. 'I pray the Lord my soul to take.' He is closer. What can I do? I will not cry. I will not cry. God send me to Hell, it must be better. I am tired. I am sore. I do not want the blood. I just want to die. He stopped on the steps. All is quiet. Maybe he fell asleep. God, do you care? Really care? If you do, why does this go on and on? Why can't you stop it? Are you real? . . . Do all dads do this to their children?

When I asked Lizzie who her father was, she said, "I don't have a father; after all, I was born when I was fourteen."

Why fourteen?

"Because that's when I stabbed Russ. Molly refused to do it, so I did. Molly was a coward, she still is; a goody-two-shoes. It felt good . . . the knife going in, breaking the flesh, the blood. . . . Sometimes I hated him; he was always after me, hitting me for doin' something. If Molly had more guts, maybe Russ wouldn't have bothered her so much. You can't judge Russ; he did what he did. That's it; he is what he is."

In women with multiple personalities, the self, overwhelmed by sudden traumata, dissociates; the process of autohypnosis creates or forges alternate selves. Because of its defensive functions, the alter allows consciousness to survive, intact, although the forms of that intactness appear as discrete compartmentalized alter personalities or fragment personalities. The creation of the alter is essential if the self is to continue living. Molly, the baby, began splitting off feelings and burying the dreadful in personalities completely detached from her. The experience of pain literally buried itself in Mute. Pain therefore remained totally inaccessible—the major consequence of dissociation. But pain was never lost. It lay within the constellation of the self, but so deeply held that its infantile core never became available to the other alters.

Molly continues her story:

It was horrible. I spent a great deal of time trying to keep the other children [her brothers and sisters] out of his reach. I remember how he dragged me by the hair, and then the headaches, the terrible nausea. I used to vomit behind the house in the woods where no one saw me or helped me. Oh, how I hated life! . . . It could have been worse; we [Molly and the other alters] could have died. There were times when I sat up in my room tugging at my hair; my mother came in and saw me with great clumps of hair laying all around me. She screamed at me to stop and then dragged me downstairs. I don't remember doing that; Elizabeth tells me that Black did all the damage to my scalp; it wasn't me, though.

Even now I sit up on the hall and I look down and I suddenly see myself with a lot of hair in my hand; other patients tell me I've been pulling my hair out. I don't know I'm doing it until Black leaves, and there I am confused by all of this. I sit there quietly, tugging at every little strand on my head until it falls out. I'm real quiet, no sounds, nothing, as if I were invisible.

Black sits in my office; I ask, "Molly, could you come out?" Nothing, just hair pulling. I repeat, "Molly, could you please come out?" Molly appears, confused, not able to say much about Black or the hair pulling. She sits there, staring blankly at the walls, with huge clumps of hair in her hand. I'm startled by all this, alarmed. Finally I ask Clear to come out. I want to know the reason behind the hair pulling.

Clear: When Molly was a kid, Russell, whenever he had the chance, grabbed her by the hair and banged her head against the wall. It was punishment. Black was created during those moments; I think it was a ritual Russell practiced before he raped Molly. Whenever Molly gets close to the memory, she finds herself with these pounding headaches; nothing helps. . . . It never seems to go away.

Whenever Molly recalled Black, what came back to her was the feeling of a headache. She literally curled up into a ball and moaned for about twenty minutes. Nothing I said reached her. Sometimes her eyes closed; sometimes she opened them without any recognition. At those moments she had the blank stare of a corpse.

Molly: I remember a brook, surrounded with willow trees. I went there to find some peace; it was the only place I escaped to. I listened to the stream. I imagined myself dissolving in it, in its clarity. That quiet sound, water flowing, gave me solitude. For a moment at least, I escaped the pain. But Mom found me; she crept up and screamed, "You lying little bitch, what the hell are you doing?" You know what she did? She stripped the willow trees and made branches into whips. She used them on me almost every day.

I asked Molly if anything could have been more terrible than her father. "We lived; he could have killed us; so there is something worse than the abuse, and that's death. We [the alters and herself] are all still alive."

If one reads Molly through Clear's eyes, Molly has no self, no being; nothing but fragments or part selves coming in and out. Or, in the words of Sylvia Gaggi describing the postmodernist approach to self: "The individual ceases to be centered in an *a priori* self, but becomes instead a locus where various signifying systems intersect" (1989: 157–58). Clear, for example, said she banished several alters to the fog because the "room was becoming too crowded" (Molly spoke of her "self" as a "room filled with people"—alters—some of whom were permanent residents and others who wandered "in and out of the fog").

I asked her, "Why the crowd?"

Clear replied, "Because Girl wanted to let everyone in." Clear argued that Girl began letting people in "from the fog" to force Mute to speak. Girl's presence in Molly was charged with emotion and knowledge, since Girl had experienced so many of Russell's beatings and rapes. It was Girl's strategy to induce Mute to give up the pain and release Molly from her amnesia by creating an intolerably crowded psychological space. Girl seemed impelled by impatience. Clear, however, pulled in a different direction.

From her point of view, Girl's strategy was wrong, because Mute would be terrified by too many people in the room. Clear, therefore, determined that Girl must banish many alters or fragments; and because Clear possessed certain authority in the constellation of alters, her will determined the strategy. Or to put it another way: Clear, who controlled the presence of the alters, was Molly's own unconscious effort to save *herself*. Girl had simply experienced too much to know what she was doing. For Clear, Girl's despair interfered with "rational thinking." So many alters made the therapeutic task extremely complex; and with too many alters to deal with, consciousness may very well have imploded. Molly's self-destructiveness intensified with the presence of hostile or negative alters, precisely the alters Girl wanted to bring inside. And it was these fragments, alters not nearly as well defined as Elizabeth, Lizzie, Maggie, or Black, that Clear insisted be kept in the fog—permanently. Girl, however, continued to insist to Clear that these alters be let in the room.

Girl's misery appeared in her wish to die. Many of the alters who lived in the fog had the power to induce Molly to commit suicide or to put herself in dangerous situations, and Clear wanted to keep these extraordinary hostile presences as far away as possible—as far out of the field of consciousness as she could. By keeping the number of alters manageable, Clear in effect contributed to, even to an extent managed, the therapeutic effort at integration.

I asked Clear if Girl was her enemy.

No. She's just a little girl who does not know the consequences of her actions. She understands pain and abuse; that's her entire world. You can't blame her; she witnessed the rapes; she saw the whole thing going on. That's quite a burden for a child; it's up to me to think for the alters, to banish to the fog and to take in from the fog. Girl simply does not know what she's doing. She's incapable of making an intelligent, much less a rational decision. Besides, I think she wants to die. But if she dies, Molly dies. And I will not let that happen.

In a case of multiple personality, there is no independent cohesive link in the self that can allow the personality to take responsibility. Everything, even seductive actions, is considered to be the work of alters, illusory presences taking shape as discrete parts, who exist independently of any controlling agency. By banishing alters to the fog, Molly, through Clear, unconsciously denies them presence and agency. It is an act of collaboration between her and other more significant alters such as Clear and Elizabeth. Banishment asserts a form of control, something of a hierarchy, and narrows the room or space that contains the alters. A less crowded room or a more manageable psychological space or internal world facilitates consolidation and cohesion. When alters lie in the fog, they are not viable. They exist as latent presences in the self, but without agency. The density of alters may create an intolerable confusion, and the profusion of self-destructive alters may lead to suicide.

It is this capacity within Molly which paradoxically keeps her alive and implicitly supports the aims of therapy. If there were no fog, the room would indeed become too crowded, particularly with hostile alters, and the very confusion of the crowd and its enormity would strangle Molly, forcing her to find a physical route, notably suicide, out of the density of her internal world.

In the year prior to Molly's admission to the hospital the room had indeed become too crowded, and Molly had tried to kill herself. It was then that Clear suggested to Molly that she find help in sorting out the crowd and locating meaning in the confusion. If she could, she might be able to close the door and send some of the more ill-defined destructive alters "back into the fog."

Molly: I don't remember the cutting or the blood; the emergency room, being stitched up, finding my way to Sheppard-Pratt: I remember none of it. Clear tells me that after I tried to kill myself she signed me into the hospital, negotiated with the emergency-room doctors; she arranged everything with Sheppard-Pratt and made the final decision to seek help.

It was in the hospital that I encountered the horror of her history and narrative.

Molly's Humiliation

Is Molly's multiple personality disorder a symbolic representation of the broken-up, fragmented, and disconnected character of modern life, a radical example of the existence of disconnectedness? Is it at the same time a dramatic plea for a sense of coherence, wholeness, and unity, an argument against the celebration of fragmentation? What is one to make of amnesiac barriers between alters, prior to the host's recognition that alters exist? The self never, at any point in time, exists as one, but always, from the very beginning, as several; yet consciousness is not aware of this "seriality." Prior to therapeutic intervention, the only understanding the self has of her multiplicity is what she describes as "blackouts," of which consciousness recalls nothing. Is the core of the self in Molly to be found in the child alter, in, for example, Little Girl and Mute? What triggers recognition?

In therapy, it is essential that the alters be brought into what might be called an intrapsychic community, with likeness and disagreements that may contribute toward the creation of a cohesive self and a coherent field. This consciousness need not be monolithic; it may be a unity representing a plurality of interests within the self, interests understood as emotions and moods. This plurality, then, may coexist not as discrete, disconnected parts but as a community of conflicting moods that possess a recognizable coherence, an identity. (That kind of plurality, however, is a much different phenomenon than the discrete alters of the multiple personality.) That consciousness had begun when I first talked with Molly.

Molly enters my office; she carries with her a can of soda pop. She sits silently for a few minutes and then starts peeling the can, like an apple. Her fingers bleed, but she continues to peel. I become alarmed and ask her to stop. But she screams, "I'm not Molly; you're talking to Elizabeth, and I won't stop until I'm finished talking. I want to tell you a story." I told her I would listen to her story only if she stopped cutting her fingers. She put down the can but said she would finish peeling it when she had finished with her story. I asked her why she had to peel the can. "Because it reminds me of what Russell did to me. It makes me feel good; besides, I have to do it. I don't know why; I only know Russell threatened to cut my fingers off if I told."

"Told what?"

He laid me down on my back. The next thing I knew Clear appeared. I felt her; she took me up to the ceiling and I sat on that ceiling face up, not paying any attention to the screams below. I knew Girl must have been there. Maybe even Miriam. And I lay face up on the woodshed's ceiling, an old corrugated-iron sheet.

. . . It was hot in the summer, real cold in the winter. If it was raining, I felt the raindrops splashing right above my face; they drowned the sounds beneath me. I dared not look. . . . Clear told me not to look; it might scare me. And that rain came down, sometimes real slowly like soft cat paws working their way across my face.

Clear told me not to look down, because if I did I might fall back and she didn't want that to happen. So Clear stayed up there telling stories, warning me not to pay attention to the noises rising up from underneath. Clear told me stories about families, mommys and daddys and children who had fun and were happy, who lived in nice homes and where daddys slept in their own rooms. She told me how monkeys got bugs in their skin and how the bugs were invited by the monkeys to be there, and how the bugs found a home, because the bugs were sad and had no home . . ., and the mommy monkey wanted the bugs to feel good and have a home and the daddy monkey wanted to protect the bugs. That's why the bugs found their way into the monkey's skin: because they were happy to be there. These daddy monkeys didn't cut up pigs in front of their children.

Finally when it was over, when Russell finished with Girl or Miriam or whomever, Clear put me to sleep. When I woke up on that bench, it was terribly painful. I hurt all over; blood was all over me. . . . I didn't know what to do or think. . . . But Clear told me to be quiet, and not disturb Russell, who sometimes slept in a chair next to the bench. She told me I should think about the stories and how good the stories made me feel. I cleaned myself up and went outside to the woods where I listened to Clear sing lullabies. I forgot what my body felt like. . . .

After Russell woke up, he took me back into the shop, sat me by the jigsaw, and threatened to cut off all my fingers if I told. He took my hand, put it on his leg and said things like, "What pretty fingers! What good caring they do! How would you feel if they weren't there? . . . If they were cut off? You won't have any fingers if you tell! Fingers bleed and your hand might fall off too."

Elizabeth/Molly continues to peel the can; her fingers have small cuts on them. They bleed. Finally Molly appears; the can is completely peeled and the pieces of metal deposited in my wastebasket.

As she leaves, Molly says Elizabeth is the poet of the group. She tells me that Clear loves Elizabeth and needs her in the room. Clear requires a poet, and Elizabeth tells the stories of alters who refuse to speak or cannot speak, or who will not come out to speak. Elizabeth is their emissary.

The Sadism of Some Alters

Several alters pushed or seduced Molly into self-destructive actions—including alters that appeared while she still lived in her father's house. The following are just a few examples:

Russell (Russell was the name of an alter *and* the name of Molly's father): He made Molly do "bad things" such as opening up the gate in the chicken coop and letting the chickens out. "Russell" set Molly up because when she reacted, Russell, *her father*, either raped her, beat her, or tortured her with the mutilation of animals.

Alfred: He seduced Molly into sexually provocative poses toward a favorité uncle. He flirted with the uncle, took his hand, put it on "his" breasts and suggested they go to the bedroom to "fool around." Clear felt that such desires were bad for Molly and banished Alfred and alters like him to the fog.

Alice: She set Molly up for sexual abuse by leaving liquor bottles out for Russell to drink. Again, Clear saw terrible danger here and persistently banished Alice to the fog. But Alice possessed, according to Clear, a vicious streak and unannounced made her way back to the room with some frequency. The other "bad" alters would also periodically show up.

Mary: In grade school Mary seduced Molly into absent-mindedly stupid or totally inappropriate actions, for example, going into the wrong classroom or wandering into the principal's office or peeking into the boys' restroom.

No-Name: No-Name closed Molly's eyes at night, held her hand, and literally blinded her to what had been going on during the day or earlier in the night. No-Name had the power to make Molly forget what happened just moments before.

Eddie: He made Molly think she was too thin or too fat and had her put on her brother's clothes, which were too small. Eddie also made her light fires and pour kerosene over her favorite dog's back. He once threw a lighted match onto the fur. The dog required several skin grafts and stayed at the veterinary hospital for several weeks. Molly, who was punished, had no recollection of burning her dog. Russell locked her up in a closet for fourteen hours without food or water. Afterward, he beat her until she bled from her legs.

When Molly turned sixteen, her father died. Clear at that time banished these alters to the fog. None has since reappeared.

Self-destructive impulses continued to torment Molly into her adulthood. Both Lizzie and Elizabeth liked to hurt her. Lizzie used oven cleaner, Elizabeth—knives and razor blades, broken bottles, the edges of soda cans. Molly's doctor suggested a skin graft to remove burn scars, but she refused. I asked her why:

Because that would have taken away all signs of Lizzie's badness. Lizzie knew she was bad, but she enjoyed listening to the oven cleaner burn her skin. It comforted her. She felt she deserved to be burned. Lizzie, of course, did not feel the pain; but I felt it when I peeled away the cleaner. It took a good piece of my skin with it each time.

Jane came out when Molly found herself in a dangerous situation or when the prospect of self-destruction seemed imminent. Yet Molly has little recollection of Jane as an earlier alter. I met Jane once. Elizabeth believes Jane to be much younger than her stated age of twenty-three. Also, according to Clear, Jane came out when Molly's father subjected her to the torture and dismemberment of animals. I met Jane after Molly had undergone a particularly stressful situation in looking for another patient who had run away from the hospital.

Jane: It's funny; the only thing Molly took from Russell when he died, the only possession, was his penknife. She spent hours sharpening it, making sure it cut the small hairs on her arm. She practiced on paper, grass, and the like. But Elizabeth did the cutting; she was the one who was out. She made small horizontal cuts over the inside of the wrist and on the inside of her arms and thighs, so small, so delicate, you had trouble seeing them.

Elizabeth cleaned up the cuts and no one ever knew. Isn't it strange? For years, Molly had been terrified of that penknife; all of us were [the alters], because we knew what Russell had done with it, how many animals he had cut, how many times during the rapes he flashed that knife in front of Molly's eyes. Isn't it odd— that what Molly chose to take from Russell after he died was his penknife, his instrument of torture?

Jane did possess power in Molly's psychic constellation. She induced action, when she believed it essential. Lizzie told me that before she stabbed Russell with the knife, Jane whispered into her ear that something had to be done to keep Russell from the children [Molly's brothers and sisters]. Although murky and never detailed in my conversations with Molly or any of the alters, Jane seemed to exercise some agency in Molly's internal world.

An Alter That Painfully Introduces Reality

Silent for years, Mute appeared (in the last two months of Molly's hospitalization) by giving intense pain to other alters. Molly herself often seemed to be in great distress; and in his dialogues with Molly's therapist, Mute described his project of slowly doling out pain to significant alters. For example, staff often found Molly curled up, gripping her legs, her face contorted in bizarre grimaces. At times she screamed but had no later awareness of these events. Except for a few observant patients and staff, no one had any idea that the person screaming or holding her legs was an alter and not Molly. Molly, however, felt the presence of Mute: she appeared exhausted; she rarely ate, because as she put it, "Food tastes of semen."

It was particularly distressing to listen to Clear describe what happened to Little Girl, an alter that during Molly's final weeks in the hospital came out with some frequency. During those moments, Little Girl/Molly found herself screaming or crying and possessed very few words to tell others what was going on. According to Clear, however, Mute finally let "all Hell break loose." This anguished presence in Molly became real, unspeakable pain. Nothing mattered but pain and its terror. His nothingness was not emptiness or the sheer vacuum of postmodernism: it was pain. Mute served as all the alters' collective Hell; they hated him, because he forced them (and himself as a critical alter in Molly's constellation) to suffer reality.

Recovering pain (flashbacks and the more intense "abreactions," the actual reliving of the trauma) destroys the affective amnesia surrounding trauma. Before Mute started depositing pain, Lizzie could be seductive and playful, fun-loving; but once Lizzie began remembering, once Little Girl's horror made its way into Molly's *body*, the masks of seductiveness or indifference vanished and the sheer terror of emotion filled the fragments of Molly's being. Mute says that Little Girl never really understood what was happening to her; she only knew that Russell liked to take her to the woods, that his voice sounded sweet while she rubbed his body with alcohol, that she threw up blood because Russell tore at her mouth and gums. She lay there, in the meadow, and did what her father ordered. But emotionally Mute took the pain; he stored it up; he locked it away.

Not having been a participant in the actual rapes, Clear could recount them and describe Molly's alter-history with little passion. Clear's flatness, her masquelike quality, often made me feel as if I were in the presence of a massive defensive system, that an impenetrable and totally armored truth lay beyond Clear, that Clear herself may have been a grim simulation of a reality I had yet to discover.

It is in Little Girl, however, that the possibility of a cohesive self, and therefore a life rooted in a continuous history, was early destroyed. Hers is a story that details the carnage of the body and self in a rural setting of extraordinary beauty. In those quiet settings, Molly could not even scream; to save herself she became entirely different persons. Little Girl persistently replaced Molly; Little Girl knew the violence. Dissociation, then, was Molly's means of survival: the power to literally tear herself away from her "being" and through a complex form of autohypnosis both to deny reality and to forge an alternate presence or consciousness replacing the already existing self.

Her father's brutality, his alcoholism and violence, gave birth in Molly's toddler-hood to totally separate selves (Little Girl and Mute) with no bridge at all to Molly. This is important: (1) Molly's multiplicity of self existed to defend her against acknowledging a terrifying emotional reality; and (2) Molly's multiplicity signified an interior world of disconnected others, in the form of alters, that performed no mirroring function. Others, for multiple personalities, are not mirrors, but free-floating histories that coalesce as isolated, noncommunicating entities. It may be years before the self comes to any awareness of her multiplicity; such knowledge as does arise requires difficult communicative bridges among the alters. Such consciousness usually accompanies the therapeutic dialectic, a process that both initiates dialogue, creates mirrors, and brings great pain.

The Death of the Alters

At our last meeting, both Elizabeth and Clear came out to say goodbye. I thanked each for her cooperation and her willingness to describe her experiences. I also expressed some curiosity as to why Elizabeth liked to peel soda pop cans. We had never explored this action, because Elizabeth seemed adamant in defending it and showed no willingness to talk about it.

Elizabeth: It's simple: I like to see blood; it makes me feel I'm
alive. Nothing else does. . . . Why not tear a styrofoam cup? It
makes no marks, draws no blood. Sometimes after Russell raped
me, I'd go to the stream and just sit there, watching the water.
Sometimes I saw my blood floating with the sticks and leaves. It
made the stream dark, and I lost the fish. I couldn't see them anymore.
I discovered I could take myself out of time. Going up to the ceiling was for special occasions. In my bedroom, or in the woods, I
pretended Russell was an animal—a pig, or a cat. He could be
furry or smooth, or even a porcupine with sharp quills sticking me.
I'd close my eyes and imagine I was somewhere else, with all these
animals crawling over me. I played with leaves and chipmunks.
Clear and I had great fun with the pretend game.

For Elizabeth, reality appeared in three different forms: (1) "here," as a kind of existential place defined by conversation about herself and the other alters; (2) the room in her head populated by the other alters; and (3) the fog. She liked the fog best, she said, because in its density (the postmodern opacity?) she found herself able to live in the land of pretend without worrying about being hurt. But she also feared being banished to the fog, because then she could not come back. To be in the fog would be too "real." I was struck here by how close Elizabeth's concept of the real was to Lacan's, if Lacan's concept be understood as the imminence of death, the real as an experience so powerful, so overwhelming, that the self only approaches it, never really touches it.

Clear, however, forbade, at least for now, Elizabeth's merging into the fog. She believed that Molly's only hope for gaining access to her own memories lay in Elizabeth's capacity for language, articulation, and, as she put it, "poetry." Elizabeth was to be the primary medium for Molly to gain access to the split-off, lost parts of her self, memories critical to Molly's survival and, therapeutically, for the integration and consolidation of an historically known self. For Clear, whatever knowledge could be gained lay in that dense population in the room. Elizabeth had been designated by Clear to tell the tale of her father's crimes.

But I also sensed in my conversations with both Clear and Elizabeth that each regarded the other with some suspicion. Both competed for a larger share of the room in the head, the space of identities that composed Molly's collective identity. The great difference between Clear and Elizabeth (and one Clear completely understood) was the fact that Elizabeth possessed an emotional connection to Molly's life. Clear existed as seer, observer, and rescuer.

For Clear, people's actions demonstrated whether they were bad or good. For example, Molly—good; Russell—bad. The bad people would be destroyed; the good people saved. Destruction took the following form: the bad people, after committing horrendous acts, decided, in their arrogance, that they had a special power enabling them to fly. But they needed wings, so they found a batch of old feathers and glued them to their arms. Eventually consumed with ambition, these birds flew blindly toward the sun. They flew too far and either were burned alive or suffocated from the heat. The dead birds then dropped back to the earth, where roving bands of rats ate whatever flesh remained on their bones.

Elizabeth once asked Clear why she refused to let Elizabeth fly to the sun, because often she had insisted that Clear kill her. Only the bad deserved to die, Clear told her. Elizabeth felt that Clear at those moments condemned her to life. For Clear, however, Elizabeth had the function of holding knowledge and communicating it to other alters and to the world.

It was Elizabeth who with some sadness was the last alter to say goodbye. In our final meeting, she said:

Girl will bring Molly happiness; Maggie, intelligence; Mute, feeling. But what will I bring her, what will I be? Clear told me I will be the person who tells the world what being multiple is like—what we have to go through, what we have gone through. And how all of us will someday return to the fog. This is what people are not capable of understanding. Each of us is real; each of us is here. Even though we all share a body, Molly's body, we are people; but all of us have to die. Clear never explained death to us, but when she says I have to wait in the fog and doesn't tell me what I have to wait for, she means I must die.

No one really understands, not the psychiatrists, not our families, that all of us are *people*. Oh, I know I'm eleven, but I've seen things, I've had horrible things done to me. I've wanted to die and disappear. But Clear is right. For Molly to live, all of us have to go back to the fog, to the land of magic and death. And when I think about that, it makes me sad; Elizabeth will have to grow up, but if I grow up, I will die.

Evil and the Postmodernists

Occasionally Baudrillard's observations on evil capture something of the horror of what the infant and child experience at the hands of the father as torturer, as marauder, the terror that lies inside of Molly. He writes, "Imagine something good that would shine forth from all the power of Evil: that's God, a perverse god who in defiance created the world, enjoining it to destroy itself" (1988: 188). Is this evil not the father who habitually and traumatically abuses, both physically and sexually, his daughter? Is this not evil, in its pure form, a man who acts as God within the confines of the regime of desire, who transgresses not only the primordial laws of incest but the very patriarchal power that creates the authority, the very canons of the civilization that gives his life its structure, meaning, and existence? Such persons may be said to embody or represent evil in Baudrillard's terms: "When insanity is victorious in every way, we have the principle of Evil" (185).

Baudrillard claims that the "universe is not dialectical; it moves toward the extremes, and not toward equilibrium. It is devoted to a radical antagonism and not to reconciliation or to synthesis." And indeed, this is the universe of the traumatized child. Certainly multiple personalities may not be understood as living in any universe that presents itself as a synthesis. Alter personalities embody extreme reactions to traumatic events; nothing is ambivalent or resolved or transcended. The presence of alters signifies the victory of cruelty, domination, and tyranny, and for such selves to come into existence is the result of a domination of a particularly horrible kind, a kind Baudrillard describes: "The principle of Evil . . . is expressed in the cunning genius of the object, in the ecstatic form of the pure object, and in its victorious strategy over the subject" (1988: 85). Here I interpolate father as object, devouring the daughter as subject. In this respect, Baudrillard's' linking of the extremes of modernity (domination and terror) and the presence of evil possesses a certain resonance in the experience of the multiple personality. What I want to emphasize, however, is that the disconnectedness celebrated by postmodern thought can itself become a form of torment and terror.

The father as phallocrat, repudiating the laws of civil society, creating evil in hidden, private spaces, lives without moral injunction. This father indifferently wanders within the space he has literally carved out of his daughter's body. Baudrillard's words are relevant: "Truly private (*privatissime*) space was the prerogative of the Prince, just as incest and transgression were the exclusive rights of kings" (158). Father/phallocrat/God imposes himself as tyrant on the body of his child; her body and consciousness become his fiefdom; his tyranny, his incest, is bound only by the limits of her flesh and the depth of her suffering. The psychological process of disconnection which follows—discrete personalities occupying the same body—is the direct consequence of this terrorizing.

Baudrillard's Surrealism and the Multiple Self

The modern world Baudrillard sees resonates with the Heraclitian view of constant movement and transformation, although movement for Baudrillard, rather than possessing a creative or novel component, generates pure repetition, simulation, illusions built on illusions, endlessly repeating copies. In this world, with its utter emptiness of value and the absence of fixed points of reference, is not the self totally lost? And would not survival of the self, its very connection with the life instinct, require some connection to meaning, an effort to find a *gestalt* that remains constant through the self's shifting constellations and moods?

The existence of the multiple personality might be understood as analogous to a surrealist drawing, in which the discrete totalities do not touch or exhibit any intrinsic connection, a compartmentalized universe without meaning or *telos*, but "there" (a very heavy "thereness"). The images are held not by any internal narrative, but by the frame of the drawing itself. The surreal is an existential *ground*.

Baudrillard sees the secret of surrealism where "the most banal reality could become surreal, but only at privileged moments, which still derived from art and the imaginary" (1988: 146). The very conditions of the multiple personality's life, the banal appearing as ordinary, day-to-day choices, conditioned responses to the hyperreal, find themselves defined by alter personalities with utterly no connection.

The boundaries of surrealist images are random, not inherently or dialectically fused. Similarly with the images (alters) of the multiple personality: no interior narrative line connects each personality; each lives within its own compartment; each one's birth depends on a specific trauma or event. Many alters are not aware of the existence of others. What holds them together is the sheer physicality of the host's body. Nothing touches; nothing makes sense, but the discrete parts, each of which seems to possess its own life and space.

This existence is surreal because to listen to the selves speaking and switching is to be in a world beyond reality, but with the impact of phenomena that are, in their own compelling way, real. This inner world, if it could be drawn, would have no coherence at all; it would be filled with a series of static images each confronting the other, with no connection to the other, with no causality, form, or structure.

Baudrillard's artist has a ground or point from which to project the surreal, a self-conscious sense of living and working with the imaginary. The artist may move in and out, from surreal back to real, from the image back to the alienation that produces the image. The multiple personality, however, has no sense of working within a reality to create an image that intensifies the experience of reality. Life itself becomes the drawing.

For Baudrillard, modern existence embodies the victory of the hyperreal; we inhabit and mediate the universe of endless production and reproduction. These phantasms and illusions, the dullness of the hyperreal, the disconnection of the surreal, the absence of intrinsic meanings and identifiable truths, surround, even define the self. It is therefore no longer possible to distinguish appearance from reality; even emotions, moods, feelings, are evanescent, darting in and out of consciousness because of the "chance" of biology and the forces of reproduction which form the substratum of social life.

For the "normal" or normalizing society, this incorporation creates a dull blandness, life as repetition, image tumbling on image. For the multiple personality, however, existence as one disembodied image following another (the hallmark of consumerism) forges not a bland conformity, the dulled sense of a self living within a world spelled out by the insanity of what appears to be sane. Rather, the disconnectedness of life brings with it a terror, a horror of existence which, because of its very origins, can never possess certainty as to what the world will look like and what the self will be. The constant switching and shifting of personalities, especially when the host becomes aware of her multiplicity, radically dislocates the self and makes it impossible to find a ground, a point from which the perception of existence reflects meaningful, sure, and certain properties.

To be multiple, then, is to live out the terms of a psychically determined surrealism, to be caught in an endlessly disintegrating process, to know nothing of continuity or wholeness. Consciousness lives not in history but in a transhistorical space of images lacking any inherent psychological or affective connection, other than the common property of defense against horror. Baudrillard speaks of the "dizziness of death . . . the allegory of death," the disintegration of the real, the evanescent quality of experience, the destruction of meaning and the utter impossibility of finding an inherent coherence or structure in reality (1988: 144–45). Is this not true for the multiple personality? Is not the real for the multiple personality a journey through experience internalized as a continually repeating process of deconstructions, where each "self" or personality, on a day-to-day basis, faces the imminence of death and annihilation?

Conclusion: Postmodernism as a Viable Philosophy of the Self?

Postmodernism's dalliance with disconnection and chaos may be either trivial, a just plain false interpretation, or, more likely, dangerously irresponsible. To suggest that persons have no connections, no histories, no cohesive selves, is literally to throw the self into a psychologically contingent world.

The postmodernist theory of multiplicity—and I do believe Baudrillard is representative in this respect—is an extreme rejection of boundary, stability, historicity, and any concept of a unitary or cohesive self. To live the life (the facts) of multiple selfhood is not to know where one self begins and others end. It is to be lost, without any sense of historical continuity to one's being. This kind of "freedom" is not liberation but enslavement to a contingent world, a frightening internal and external set of perceptions which have the power to impose serious, if not deadly, emotional fragmentation and psychological dislocation.

It is a mistake to dismiss the experiences of women with multiple personality disorders as so pathological that the cases can be ignored or dismissed as aberrant. These are true instances of living with multiple identities: an empirical testament, as it were, to what living multiple means as a set of existential facts. Multiple selves are graphic representations of a multiplicity produced by powerful political and psychological currents, specifically patriarchy and domination, that exercise an enormous influence over culture and modern social practices. In this respect, multiplicity is symptomatic of what the French psychoanalytic feminists see as the worst of modernity: acts of domination ("this solidarity between logocentrism and phallocentrism"—Cixous, in Cixous and Clément 1986: 65) that have little or no respect for the body, the intellect, or the self.

If multiplicity of self derives from a paternal domination literally fixed in a kind of Hobbesian natural condition, if multiplicity is the toxic outgrowth of abuse by parental authority and power (in the cases I am aware of),[2] then its origins lie not in a celebration of difference but in the noxious and debilitating endgames of a corrupt modernity. That is the paradox, and one that distinguishes the French feminists from such postmodernists as Baudrillard: postmodernism as a philosophy celebrates a form of human experience that in its most vivid representations derives from the most corrupt reaches of modernity. How can this possibly be an "advance," either psychologically or politically? Or, as Cixous puts it: "Philosophy is constructed on the premise of woman's abasement. Subordination of the feminine to the masculine order, which gives the appearance of being the condition for the machinery's functioning. . . . What would happen to logocentrism, to the great philosophical systems, to the order of the world in general if the rock upon which they founded this church should crumble?" (Cixous and Clément 1986: 65).

Finally, if the postmodernist notion of self and multiplicity is simply not a restatement of liberal pluralism or of rights-based individualism with an emphasis on play, if we take it seriously (and the postmodernists or those postmodernists who do not sound like reborn liberal individualists intend it to be taken seriously), then the most striking examples or illustrations of multiplicity are to be found in human beings, specifically female human beings, who are the

---

[2]Cixous' "choir swollen by sobs and silences, breathless gasps, hysterics' coughs" (Cixous and Clément 1986: 107), or Clément's "This history, locked up tight between father and son, includes nothing that touches woman; moreover, it is invented to get rid of her" (ibid.: 56).

tragic victims of patriarchal domination. That is the real sickness, the real pathology: a set of assumptions about women, the ownership of their bodies, the disrespect for their humanity, and the cruelty exercised against children. That indictment is etched into these fractured creations of mind. It makes no sense to idealize a form of human experience whose most dramatic etiology lies in some of the most perverse representations of human desire.

6 · SATAN'S DAUGHTERS: POWER, EVIL, AND THE ORGANIZATION OF THE MULTIPLE SELF

Psychoanalytic views of what the self is depend on clinical observations that describe conditions of real distress. The experiences of selves in pain demonstrate how important it is to think of the self as a malleable structure (Winnicott's "going on being"), free to change and choose, but nonetheless a self distinguished not by its fragmentation but by the need to live and survive with fixed points of reference, stable boundaries between self and other, and a firm sense of one's identity as an active agent in the world.

In this respect, the self might be thought about as a series of impressions and representations transformed and altered through experiences hardly accessible to rational understanding. A cohesive identity, depending on its preverbal (or what psychoanalytic object-relations theorists call "preoedipal") influences may produce expansive and creative dynamics or, tragically, may find itself abused by disintegrative forces that unhinge consciousness. Clinical evidence of that inner derangement, specifically traumatization of the core self, suggests that the self is more than a reflection of whatever historical and social practices may be imposed on it (the Foucaultian postmodern position). The self forms, but the process of "forming" creates a core, an essential inwardness, that may not be accessible to consciousness but may, in fact, drive the identifications that link consciousness with the external world.

It is this formative and dynamic core that has been shattered in multiple personalities by the invasive actions of paternal power and the sadism of repeated sexual and physical abuse. That "power" takes on a collective or public dimension when it is associated with the actions of cults, specifically satanic cults that have produced survivors with severe dissociative disorders. Paternal incest, coupled with the group practices of satanic cults, adds yet another terrifying level to the problematic of multiplicity as it is formed or induced by group desire.

The Terrorized Self as Group Self

Evidence for the existence of satanic cults is scanty; systematic exploration of their effects and structure is almost impossible, because, obviously, access to cult practice is jealously guarded. What happens, then, inside the cult is often derivative information, coming mainly from survivors. Knowledge of those rituals and their effects emerges through the intense emotional abreactions of survivors. Empirically, the cult's existence is confirmed through survivor accounts; cults are a reality known to the "outside" primarily through what its victims say. Clinicians have been seeing increasing numbers of women who have been brutalized by the rituals and practices of satanic cults. A consequence of that brutalization lies in the phenomenology of multiple personality disorder.

It is a gruesome form of multiplicity, because so much of the trauma is written on the body as self-torture and disfigurement. I had a great deal of difficulty with the two cases I shall describe; the facts of physical and sexual abuse by themselves are frightening and disturbing. But to listen to the stories that situate such abuse not only within the family but also in the group environment of the cult adds a totally new dimension to what it means to experience brutality and the force of terrorizing power.

Clinicians dispute the authenticity of stories of cult abuse. Some argue that it actually happens; others, that it is not really as dramatic as the victims make it out to be; still others suggest that internally held fantasies complicate and confabulate survivor accounts, making the abuse more horrifying than what "actually" happened. But what did actually happen? If even a small percentage of what I heard is "true," that is terrible enough. If one believes such cults do exist, and I do, the children of cult members, particularly female children, are subject to some kind of group-defined ritual abuse. What I learned from clinicians and saw in these patients convinced me of this fundamental fact.

The cult produces terror; it thrives on terror; it is an instrument of terror; the cult as it finds its way into the mental hospital terrorizes. What one does not understand or see brings fear. The unknowable (for ultimately how can the existence of the cult or its agents be confirmed?) becomes the third person in the therapeutic process. The cult experience also transforms into a form of power which exercises a significant presence in the self's construction (as a reason for the production of multiple personalities) and in the institutional matrix that treats multiple personality disorder.

In my sixteen years of research at Sheppard-Pratt, I have never before encountered such a confounding and ultimately unknowable form of human experience. I was shocked by the stories I heard; I could not fathom the damage women imposed on their bodies as the result of so-called cult programming: massive injuries to heads, wrists, arms—physical self-torment and abuse written as disfigured texts and stigmata on the body. What is one to make of huge blood clots on the side of the face caused by banging the head against marble fireplaces; or gashes in the flesh, grim reminders of aborted suicide attempts; or screams coming from a patient who insists that she be trundled up in restraints in order to keep her from killing herself on the anniversary of a satanic holiday; or stories of babies' blood being drunk, or of limbs severed at nightly rituals that happened twenty years previously?

Even books on cult experiences were not sufficient to prepare me for the horror of these narratives. There is a reality to the terror in these stories absent in the narratives of schizophrenics or borderline patients. Physical abuse, and the history of that abuse as it appears in the self-destructiveness of children terrorized by cults, pushes the issue of what the self is into an entirely new category.

Schizophrenia and borderline conditions derive, in terms of psychological etiology, from a profound emotional neglect and insensitivity, so that a massive failure of the emotional system itself results. (In the case of schizophrenic patients, chemical and biological elements play an obviously important role.) With the cult-abuse victim an additional factor radically complicates the picture: a group calling itself a cult practices violent rituals in the darkness. If ever the face of power shows an almost pure evil, it is in satanic cults and their practices. The survivor through recollection embodies or represents what the cult is as a practice of evil. And those recollections are filled with horror.

KIMBERLY: Ritual Degradation and the Emergence of Multiple Selves

Kimberly, twenty-two years old, believed that she had been programmed to return to a local satanic cult on a specific day in 1990; at such time she would be inducted as a full member. Further, during the initiation or induction rites she would perform a blood sacrifice with her father, whom Kimberly knew to be the cult's high priest and who had sexually abused her from the age of six. As early as the age of four, Kimberly recalled that she had been taken to cult rituals where she drank human blood, slaughtered animals, and participated in ritual dismemberment of unsuspecting, drugged victims. Both Kimberly's mother and father worked in high-paying professional jobs. Kimberly's therapy at Sheppard involved two interdependent objectives: to try to "treat" the multiplicity of her personality and to help her to reach some kind of understanding that would release her from "preprogrammed" messages demanding her return to the cult.

The group of persons calling themselves a cult, who gather for the purpose of worshiping Satan, programmed or brainwashed Kimberly to believe that she is bad, but not bad in the conventional sense. The rituals were designed to convince her of the worthlessness of Christian concepts and to instill in her the greatness of satanic practices; the mechanics of induction included terror, drugs, and programming. The process occurred over a number of years; Kimberly had been taught that badness held virtue; and in its rituals the cult attacked and reviled Judeo-Christian notions of goodness, virtue, and worth.

What the cult members, the high priest, and other functionaries did not know was that the little girl, the preteen, and then the teenager standing before them was not Kimberly, but a number of different alters that had been created over the years to screen the terror. It was only through her alters and their abreactive experience that Kimberly eventually arrived at an emotional knowledge of this violent "past." And dialogue with her alters did not begin until her hospitalization. Each day brought Kimberly a new revelation, a new horror; in meeting and speaking with her alters, she confronted her past, as if she were seeing herself for the first time. It is impossible to convey the intensity of Kimberly's pain and revulsion at what she discovered.

Kimberly's personality had fractured under the terror of what she witnessed and what was done to her. Psyche and body, perception and feeling, personality trait and persona—all separated, and the fractures or traumas produced separable personalities. (Alters may hold more than one trauma; there may even be several "part alters" who are not completely separate.) Each personality developed its own unique traits; each was born at a specific time; and each reflected a birth caused by a violent invasion of body and psyche. Kimberly's "self" imploded; what emerged over the years were variations on a self. But each variation was a secret from the others. No one alter had the power or capacity to forge a unitary or completed self (although usually there is an alter who has an overview of the self's suffering and some knowledge of the other alters' existence). The following is a partial list of Kimberly's alter personalities: Nea (2), Tink (4), Morgan (4), Jenny Precious (5), Toby (5), Emily (6), Rage (6), Lillian (7), Lucy (8), Dylan (8), Leda (8), Max (8), Joe (9), Ingrid (9), Laura (9), Miranda (9), Elizabeth (17), Gloria (17), Victoria (17), Ruthie (18). Max appeared because he thought that as a male he could protect Kimberly from the terrible things happening to her.

Kimberly feared that through a phone call or a "plant" on the unit or in the hospital a trigger word or sign might induce her to leave the hospital and return to the cult. If this programming were not activated, that is, if Kimberly never heard the word or saw the sign, a secondary program would kick in, forcing her to commit suicide either by hanging herself on her closet door or by slicing her veins open with her fingernails in a warm shower. Kimberly therefore felt that she was doomed: either the cult would find her or she would commit suicide. Kimberly's fear, compounded by the staff's paranoia (How would this trigger word find Kimberly? Should she accept phone calls? Were strangers on the unit cult members?), had an enormous impact on her treatment.

Kimberly's treatment team, the hall staff, and other patients became caught up in an environment of terror. No longer was only Kimberly's internal self involved; Kim's existence found itself associated with criminal activities and paranoid precautions that suggested a Stalinist nightmare rather than the therapeutic milieu of a "containing" psychiatric presence.

For example, one morning Kim's therapist tripped over a dead rabbit on her own doorstep; she was convinced that she had been followed on a trip halfway across the state; certain items were missing from her car; she received mysterious, hang-up phone calls. Nervousness among staff increased; fewer staff volunteered for the night shift; female staff refused to walk alone into the parking lot at night. I saw a fear on the hall I had never seen before.

Specialists told me that in the treatment of multiple personality disorder in cult cases intimidation of therapists could occur. Yet it was impossible to diminish the level of paranoia; the walls of the asylum had been breached; treatment had been poisoned by reality. Patients, staff, even some hospital administrators felt unprotected and vulnerable. Suddenly books, police reports, compendia of newspaper articles on cults materialized; staff whispered in the hallways; I was handed a sheaf of photocopied papers (material on cults) by a therapist who made me swear I would not take it out of the hospital. Many wondered if they should change their phone numbers or find dummy addresses or even take secret vacations from work, to throw off any would-be pursuers. People were careful whom they spoke with, and a few staff members refused to talk with me about anything having to do with cults because they suspected that they and I were being "watched."

It was a difficult period: Was the entire staff regressing to a Kleinian paranoid/schizoid state? Was the treatment environment itself no longer distinguishable from what was being treated? To what extent had Kim's treatment team and therapist become caught up in a collective madness that functioned something like *folie à deux*? Or had the "group" itself succumbed to a debilitating mass delusion?

The more I thought about these questions, the more sensitive I became to deviations in my own "normal," expectable environment. On the one-hour drive from my home to the hospital, I "saw" cars following me; each morning and evening (on the drive back) I searched the road for these cars, and when I "spotted" them I turned off the highway and waited for them to pass. Or I hid until I would be pretty sure they had missed me. I saw objects in places other than the places I thought I had put them. My office door at the hospital was unlocked when I was convinced it had been locked. Suspicious characters lurked around the hospital, in front of my home, and outside my office at the university. In the middle of a lecture, a stranger walked through the auditorium; I "knew" he was a cult plant.

Kim's presence at the hospital unleashed a whole host of demons. Were these demons real? Strangely, it didn't matter: what mattered is what people felt and believed.

A Past Brought to Life

Sometimes Kim recalled terrifying experiences; she told me that the alters sent her these images. On other occasions an alter would be out acting as a conduit for the "forgotten" memory. For example, Ruthie describes how she feels:

I want to rip out my slimy guts . . . shot through with a twelve-gauge shotgun . . . carved up into little pieces. . . . I know there's murder out there . . . they're waiting for me, behind the bushes. . . . Sometimes I want to rip my penis off . . . I hate it. . . . I want to see what's underneath . . . if there is anything underneath . . . I'm trying not to be murdered, but it is like living in a poisonous smoke . . . a fetus closed up in a fluid screaming not to be born . . . death and choking. . . . I feel it . . . it's inside me . . . but then I'm the Devil's daughter . . . Satan's child . . . with a gigantic prick. . . . I torture . . . I hate the world . . . I look around me and all I see is filth. . . . I want to tear it all out, all of it, the slime and decay of the world, to drown it, burn it up, let it wither and die. . . . If I could cut my insides out, if I could find a butcher knife large enough to do it, I would dig a hole inside myself, so deep, nothing would be left of me. . . . My guts would spill to the ground, let the dogs eat it.

Or Leda, a hostile alter, tells me that she belongs to the cult and wishes to demonstrate her loyalty to her father and his violence.

It [her father hurting her, raping her] makes me feel good; no one here [the alters, particularly the little ones, living inside the "house" in Kim's head] understands that. . . . I want to do what he tells me; I want him to hurt me. . . . I want my father to lie on top of me. . . . I like it when he hits me . . . when he pushes inside me.

Or Lucy. She has a flashback; she sits in front of me; her eyes change. Terror grips her face; she screams in pain. She tells me her genitals are being probed with electric wires. She asks me to make "them" stop; I tell her I cannot; she implores me: "Please, please, it hurts so much, please make them stop; I'm terrified." I ask Kim to come out: Lucy is in pain; will Kim please come out! After several minutes, Kim finally reappears; I leave the room, shaking, sick to my stomach.

Kim believes that her mother may have been an unwitting member of the cult itself or at least programmed to forget the abuse taken by and given by children. Further, many of Kim's alters do not want to leave the hospital; the younger ones feel that it is the safest place they have ever been. Each wishes to stay because they fear that to be in the "world" again will bring pain. At least inside the "house" in Kim's head, they find security, and the house is protected by the hospital.

The treatment environment provides an almost maternal security. Emily tells me that the hospital is the only home she has ever had. Leda, on the other hand, urges Kim to hurt herself, to cut her wrists; she screams that Kim is bad and needs to die. Clearly Leda, and to some extent Ruthie, possesses vicious sadistic qualities that work against the interests of almost all the alters in Kim's internal "house." Because Leda's loyalties lie with her father, she refuses to reveal cult secrets; she also hates Kim, because Kim sides with the "hospital." Leda sees the hospital as destructive of the interests of the cult, which of course it is. Kim tells me that cult members go to extraordinary lengths to protect their identities. "After all, it's a religion, and like all religions, if you violate the faith, there is some form of punishment."

Toby, a frightened five-year-old girl, carries in her body and language the fear, the dislocation, the horror of living through brutality. It is clear that Toby is an alter who was out during much of the early sexual abuse, including that at cult rituals. She speaks in fragments: "I secret . . . safe here from bad people?" In addition, Toby writes backward; it is a mirror image. Her script, placed directly in front of a mirror, can be read. Without the help of a mirror, it is indecipherable; Kim, however, reads Toby's words directly from script: "They make me hurt . . . burns . . . pain comes . . . pain screams." But Toby feels safe when "inside" [that is, inside the house in Kim's head]; many alters know her and provide her comfort.

But I no secret from Inside . . . I like Inside . . . Big Scary . . . Soon . . . March 29 [the day Kim feels she will be kidnaped and taken back to the cult] . . . I o.k. now . . . Daddy . . . mean . . . eyes look funny. . . . scary . . . he act crazy. [In relation to Marie-Anne, a protector angel, Toby says] old lady help us . . . soft . . . say soft words . . . hold us . . . she say different words, but not scary [like, for example, Leda].

Several alters write in Kim's notebook. Elizabeth: "My name is Elizabeth; I am responsible for the neat structure of the Inside. I like things to be neat and organized." Or Aldebaran: "I am the Spock-like[1] entity. I am nameless and ageless; I am the seer and the Knower. . . . I am the dream-giver and the analyzer." Both Elizabeth and Aldebaran exercise more power in the constellation than do the

---

[1] Based on Mr. Spock, the *Star-Trek* character.

others, but even they are incapable of controlling Rage, who has a power independent of even the most omniscient protector or rescuer personality.

In the house in Kim's head, all the "kids" (Toby, Lucy, Nea, Tink, and so on) live in a big bedroom; the older ones live on the floor below. Joe sleeps with the little ones to protect them. From time to time, a dark form appears out of the cellar. Aldebaran describes the form as "The Father." When the children see "The Father," they scream. And the house in Kim's head transforms into a place of sheer terror.

Each alter in the house has a context. For example, Dylan, five years old, periodically sends flashbacks to Kim. Elizabeth, seventeen, is prim and proper, with a talent for organization and understanding. Emily, six, was another alter out during much of the battering. When Lucy, eight [Kim tells me], looks down in her lap she sometimes sees a baby and blood and says to herself, "I'm too young to have a baby." Vivian, an innocent-looking child of seven, shows a dreamy kind of smile. She is different from the other alters her age: she talks more slowly and sits with her legs curled up. Dylan grins and is babyish; Lucy frowns a lot; and Toby with a huge dimple in her chin constantly frowns. Joe slouches and projects a hostile attitude. He talks in an English accent, and, according to Kim, is also a reliable protector.

All the alters, with a few exceptions such as Toby, speak of "The Father," not Daddy, or Dad. The phrase, coming from the alters, possesses a brutal quality—a presence of dread, fear, power, rather than comfort or protection. It was certainly not an image of a kindly or caring father. Emily constantly speaks of "lots of hurt between my legs." Toby also refers to "hurt . . . between legs."

Toby's Torture and Degradation

The following is a dialogue between a mental health worker (Debra) and Toby. Kim wrote it down immediately afterward; Debra assured me that it was a remarkably accurate reconstruction of their conversation. Keep in mind that Debra is speaking with a scared five-year-old girl.

D: How are you feeling?

T: In flashback it scary to hear name called . . . they put drug in, and then up . . . made her drink . . . then hurt came . . . no drugs here? . . . no drugs? . . . scary . . .

D: You won't have to take any drugs you don't want to; drugs here are to calm you down; so you have no need to worry.

T: But flashback has to come . . . can't come out of flashback until it over . . . flashback hurts . . . the fires . . . sharp things . . .

D: I understand that; but I'll keep you grounded here; it's o.k. to talk about it and to remember it.

T: Lots of hurt between legs . . . feel bad now . . .

D: It's not happening now; have you met your therapist? Do you know who she is? [Debra is not sure that Toby has been "out" during any of the therapy sessions.]

T: No doctors were hurt? . . . Inside . . . show me her . . .

D: I don't understand, inside what?

T: Inside . . . people [alters living in "house" inside Kimberly] . . . show me her [Kim's therapist].

D: [Toby starts to cry.] Would you like to tell me why you are crying?

T: Doctor man . . . there with bad people . . . he say hold her . . . give me drug to make me not move . . . they hold me down . . . spread legs, put wires between legs . . . make between legs hurt [Toby starts to scream] . . . it . . . the thing between my legs . . . it sounds like burning . . . it burns, help me, it burns!

D: It wasn't your fault . . . the hurt. . . . but it won't happen now . . . ; you're safe here.

T: Now I told, I be in trouble . . . they come after me . . . angry . . .

D: No; you're safe here . . . it's o.k. to talk about things . . . you're safe . . . they can't get to you anymore . . . the doors are locked . . . we check anyone who comes in . . . [Notice how Debra accepts the existence of the cult-abuse narrative as truth; at this point the reality of the event becomes the pivotal therapeutic position. It is not a question of fantasy or delusion; therapy treats perverse human action.]

T: Now . . . I told, I be in trouble . . . they open my mouth . . . put stuff in it . . . tastes bad . . . make me throw up . . . they say no tell . . . pushing between my legs . . . big thing . . . Oh, how it hurts. . . .

D: But you're safe . . . please let us help you . . . no one here wants to hurt you . . .

T: They make us forget, so we not tell . . . but now remember . . . why now? why now all the pain again?

D: I don't know why you're remembering now, but you're in a protected place and people won't hurt you . . . you can be sure of that . . . People here want to help you.

T: Why they [the cult] do that? We try to be good, try to be quiet. . . . but they hurt . . . keep hurting us all the time.

D: Some people are just very sick; and it's terrible they were able to do that to you. . . .

T: They [the cult] come to get me?

D: No, you're safe here; the doors are locked, no one can get in without telling who they are.

T: We . . . we all good girls . . . why Daddy hurt us; we good . . . no hurt anybody . . . ["we" being the alters inside the house].

D: Yes, all of you are good.

T: Nobody loved us; Daddy say he hate us, he never want us, but he tell others . . . inside . . . the girls . . . he love them . . . Daddy he take long needles . . . put them inside us; . . . my peepee, it bleeds; we go see doctor; doctor and daddy speak to each other; doctor put bandages on us, down there; it hurts so much; can't even go peepee . . . Daddy take off bandages when we get home, then he take matches out of drawer; put matches on skin; oh, how it burns . . . hurt so much . . . scream . . . Daddy, don't, please don't, stop it, please stop it . . . Daddy he laugh . . . then doctor come again . . . to house . . . put something on it from a tube . . . then feel better . . . Daddy hits us . . . screams not to tell anyone; doctor, he know . . . he daddy's friend . . . next time we see doctor, doctor alone with us . . . doctor takes down his pants and puts something into my bottom; pushes it hard; it hurts me; I scream for doctor to stop; he just laughs . . .

To listen to such stories is to witness a depravity in human nature which substitutes torture for empathy, cruelty for love, and hatred for compassion. Kimberly herself would periodically experience the flashbacks that drove Toby's narrative. Yet more often than not the abreaction (reliving the horror) came through the alters. Kimberly served as the conduit, the place or consciousness where these memories eventually emerged. To live with such horrors is to be in the midst of the Hobbesian "war of all against all." Each memory held a violence that had, at one time, smashed the very core of Kimberly's being. No refuge existed: the exercise of power brought not peace but continuing war and degradation.

Twin Alters

Kimberly contained within her several pairs of "twin" alters, personas with radically opposed personality traits but who were born at the same time (screens for specific traumas). I had encountered twins before in other patients, but never such a systematic group. Conversation within Kimberly's head with any one twin provoked the other into an immediate counterdialogue; Kimberly therefore found herself repeatedly preoccupied with often vicious and hostile debate, trying to mediate the competing interests of these strongly drawn oppositions. The following "list" is as Kimberly wrote it:

Age	Name	Relationship	Harm	Traits
4	Morgan Aldebaran	linked	abuse	serious emotionless/intelligent/analytical
6 6	Emily Rage	twins	abuse	extremely physically hurt full of rage
8 9	Lucy Laura	linked	cult	terrified was "evil," now remorseful, sad
5 2	Jenny Precious Nea	linked	cult/abuse abuse	traumatized mind preverbal senses
17	Gloria Victoria	linked	gang rape	an artist; ashamed, feels reviled tough; despises all males; may be a lesbian
9	Miranda	linked	cult	was programmed; now feels betrayed and sad

Age	Name	Relationship	Harm	Traits
	No-name			programmed; wishes to return to cult
17	Elizabeth Marie-Anne		abuse	intelligent; detached, organized very conforting, spiritual, like a mother

Note the opposing element in each pair's personality: Morgan, the serious, empathic presence; Aldebaran, omniscient, without emotion, purely rational. Emily, the hurt little child, retiring, withdrawn; Rage, outward and full of expressive anger. Lucy, terrified, frightened, existing in a state of continuing dread, but Laura, remorseful, sad, even at times grieving. Jenny Precious, a traumatized mind, pure ego, existing in a kind of linguistic horror; Nea, the toddler, never speaks but contains within her an omnipresent fear produced by abuse. Gloria and Victoria were both victims of a gang rape; one appears as an artist, ashamed, feels reviled but extremely sexy and passive; Victoria, tough, despises all males, acts much "rougher" than Gloria, has, according to Kimberly, "lesbian" tendencies. Miranda, linked with a no-name presence, feels programmed, now sees herself as betrayed and sad, wants to get as far away from the cult as possible; no-name, however, is still programmed, wants to return to the cult. Elizabeth, intelligent, detached, and organized, quite rational and "above it all," yet no expression of compassion or caring; and Marie-Anne, very comforting, possessing spiritual qualities, acts toward all the alters like a mother: the younger alters want Marie-Anne to wrap her arms around them.

Kimberly's Flight from Sheppard-Pratt

Kimberly left the hospital a few months after she arrived. She flew to a destination unknown to me, to a treatment center specializing in cult victims. Her therapist, her treatment team, and the hall administrator believed that her therapy had been compromised, that the apparent intimidation made it impossible to pursue a course of therapy beneficial to Kimberly. Further, the treatment team worried about Kimberly's safety and their own safety, because they were convinced that cult members knew that she was a patient at Sheppard-Pratt. Treatment could not proceed in an environment of terror.

Sometime later I asked Kimberly's therapist how treatment was going at the new center. The therapist told me she did not know; she was not in contact with the center, nor would she be in contact with it. Kimberly disappeared into time, but the fear and paranoia she brought with her remained on the unit. It had indeed been a trauma not only for Kimberly and her alters but for the entire treatment organization. On the day before she left, Kimberly told me, "I don't know what will happen to me, but I do know the young ones are crying all the time; they are afraid; they ask me if they will live. Or will they all be murdered? I don't know what to say. . . . What will become of us?"

NORA: Satanic Abuse and the Embodiment of the Will to Die

Nora is a twenty-four-year-old college-educated young woman from a wealthy family in the East. Her father is a distinguished professional in his town. Married when she was twenty-one, Nora is the mother of a two-and-a-half-year-old girl. When I met her, she was in the process of working out the final terms of her divorce. Her parents never visited her in the hospital; her husband wanted to ban Nora from seeing their child. Nora maintained that her husband had sexually abused their daughter. Not only was Nora's past a horror, but her present was swamped in difficulties that even a relatively well-integrated self would have found overwhelming.

Beset by anxieties over custody, her divorce, and the abreactive experiences of cult memories, Nora's presence in the hospital was marked by almost daily occurrences of self-destructive violence. I have never spoken with a patient who so dramatically registered on her body the torment of her inner self—or, in Nora's case, her multiple selves. Her anoretic body ravaged by starvation diet, marred and disfigured by cutting and banging, Nora appeared as both victim and executioner. She existed or, better, survived in a realm of pure despair.

JMG: You say you've hit rock bottom?

N: I'm below the rocks . . . all I need is a 38 . . . my brains, splattered on that wall . . . I just don't want to live . . . everything is empty . . . life . . . nothing means anything to me . . . pain, all around me . . .

Nora's subtlety in personality shift was extraordinary. Although I found little evidence of discrete, isolated personalities, shifts appeared in tone and inflection, the movement of eyebrows, voice pitch, imperceptible gestures; and Nora's therapist assured me that she had discovered two male personalities, a four-year-old little girl, a detached omniscient presence, an angry, enraged teenager, and a remorseful, withdrawn, and sad eight-year-old. Nora refused, in my conversation with her, to name the personalities. For a previous therapist she had created names, although she told me that these were inventions to please the therapist.

Nora confounded me; my experience with multiple personalities had not prepared me for such subtle shadings in alter or part-alter shifts. The hospital specialist in multiple personality disorder assured me that indeed, although Nora's personalities were difficult to see, they did exist. In the eighteen months I spoke with her, what impressed me were not separable personalities (which remained blurred in my vision of her "self"), but the immense weight and horror of her experience and her great courage in dealing with an internal world shattered by physical, sexual, and ritual abuse. What I saw, then, was not so much a "classic" case in multiple personality disorder (although I believed her therapist's view that Nora had discrete personalities) but a monumental struggle against a life defined by the presence of death, torture, and power.

Her therapist did convince me that the differences in mood, affect, gesture, and clothing revealed multiplicity; she detected alter shifts simply by the clothes Nora wore. If she wore her baseball cap, she was one personality; if she had on a certain shirt or blouse, she was a demanding fourteen-year-old adolescent; if she wore a certain kind of pants or dress, she was a tough nine-year-old boy or a shy, retiring six-year-old girl. Yet, unlike the cast of alters in Molly and Kimberly, who seem striking by virtue of narratives indicating distinguishable personalities, the vividness of Nora's universe lay in

the grim facticity of her physical body, her embodied self as register-
ing a continuing history of pain, abuse, and torture.

Each time I went to speak with Nora, I had the premonition that
I would see, etched on her body, either in bruises or cuts, the narrative reality of her past. It was almost as if her self-identity or identities appeared not only in language but in the very physical disfigurement produced by the abreactive memories of her physical and
sexual abuse.

The Body as Text for the Depravity of Power

Is it possible to link the experiences of women such as Nora with
a broader, more bureaucratized politics of terror which takes shape
in political institutions and traditions? Is such depravity a part of
human nature, a product or legacy of peculiar fault lines in the human psyche which emerge, like lava, in collective forms of human
destruction? What is the cult if not collective behavior? And what is
the victim if not a scapegoat or an object used to gratify the twisted
logics and needs of group desire?

These victims may be extreme instances of sadistic patterns flowing through human and political experience, vivid, numinous examples of the endgames of human brutality, which is itself an outgrowth of actions gratifying some form of desire. Satanic cults,
which have existed for centuries, and their victims suggest a more
ominous presence in a collective self distinguished by its mur-
derousness and disregard for human life. Indeed, if there is a connection between the politics of terror and Nora, it may lie in that
bizarre form of the gratification of desire, the blood ritual,[2] an atavis-
tic throwback that appears in the frenzied annihilation of victims
and the detached, almost schizoid, obliviousness to the suffering required for such "gratifications."

Nora hurt herself in a number of ways: the imminence of satanic
holidays (usually following Christian holidays such as Easter and
Christmas) brought about intense abreactive experiences. In emo-

---

[2]See Alford's (1992) fascinating analysis of the phenomenon in the context of classical
Greek tragedy.

tionally reliving specific instances of cult abuse, she was there: she may have been in the hospital ward physically, but her psychological presence lay in these satanic moments and in the horror of their ritual events. That reliving provoked physically destructive actions: the cutting and skinning of her ankles, cutting and slicing her breasts, banging her head and face on concrete surfaces. Nora on one occasion (a Halloween eve) tried to commit suicide by slicing her throat, arms, and neck with a piece of broken glass.

During a week preceding a satanic holiday she had been in and out of a local emergency room five times. If she were not under twenty-four-hour suicide observation or in the quiet room, Nora would find some excuse to disappear, if for only a moment. She might be found in the bathtub, slicing at her wrist with the tab of a soda can, or on a window ledge in her room, figuring out how to fall on her head, or smashing a bottle on the bathroom floor so she could swallow the fragments.

Nora believed that she had been programmed by the cult to commit blood sacrifices. She convinced herself that, if she continued to live, eventually she would leave the hospital and the cult would find her, forcing her into depravities she could not even imagine. It was her firm conviction that to preserve the lives of others, particularly her daughter's (because she might be programmed even to bring her little girl into the cult), she (Nora) must die. To live meant she might be enlisted to initiate unspeakable horrors. Further, she believed that because the hospital was committed to keeping her alive, she might have to leave the hospital and find a way to die. Yet the tiny fragment of her being that wanted to live evolved around her daughter and the possibility that "some day" she might be able to establish a normal life with the only human being who she felt loved her.

Nora, then, lived by two cravings or drives: the will to die and the will to care for her daughter. Each, of course, was mutually exclusive, but each was pursued with diligence and ferocity.

Nora lived in constant fear that a cult member might kidnap her from the hospital, force her to abduct her daughter, and then return her to the cult where she would be transformed into a high priestess of murder. For this reason she desperately wanted to remain in the hospital. Other times, when the will to die was ascendant, Nora plotted escapes from the hospital and imagined bloody suicides, involving dismemberment and vivisection. Depending on which "will" drove her, Nora considered her home to be either the hospital or a house of death she populated in her imagination with various versions of suicide. Each "room" in this house contained a unique suicide scenario. She envied Elaine, a former patient who jumped off a five-story building and killed herself, and Sandra, who drowned herself in Baltimore's Inner Harbor.

In her abreactions, Nora goes back to the woods and forest where cult abuse and repeated rapes took place. She is there with cult members, their masks, costumes, chants. During these times she may request restraints because she fears if she were not restrained, she might kill herself. On one occasion she managed to wriggle out of leather restraints (she had been literally tied into a chair at her request) and climbed up on a marble fireplace mantle. In her perception (what she was experiencing), the mantle transformed into a tree where she had sat during cult practices. When staff managed to talk her down, she, in her mind, stood naked at the cult site. Staff became the cult-member persecutors—the high priest exercising terrifying force on her body: piercing her genitals with pins, sticking electric wires into her ears, shooting burning fluids up her nose and anus, and on and on. It would often take Nora hours to return from these experiential flashbacks; and to find her way back to the "present" was, as she described it, "like making my way upward through a fifteen-mile-long cave of horrors."

Nora told me:

Cults use children to perform rituals; they cut each other up, but the real deadly stuff is done by adults to children. That is the real tragedy; and these rituals, those places. . . . I travel there in my head before these satanic holidays. . . . Why do I go there? . . . I don't know; I think maybe it's because I've been programmed . . . who knows? . . . But I'm there . . . by the stone, with the knives in my hand, with hooks being put up me . . . it's too horrible . . . I can't stand it . . . I see it now . . . keep away from me! . . . Please, no! . . . No, don't, don't! . . . Please don't!

In this particular instance, Nora came back relatively quickly, but the force of her literally "being there" left me shaking.

For Nora, the memory of these events is dimmed by drugs that were given to her as a participant; all recollection is filtered by drug-induced memories and screens of fifteen, twenty years earlier.

During her childhood, Nora's parents persistently ignored her; often she was locked in a closet when they left the house. An older brother raped her for years; she had a nanny who beat her and forced her to eat foods she hated. Early in life, Nora learned what she called the "will to die":

It was the stuff of my life; the wish to die defined how I felt . . . from the time my brother threw me on the floor and raped me, to the hours I spent in the closet when my parents went out, to what I had to endure during cult practices. Nothing in my life had anything to do with life—I mean the things people really enjoy and do . . . pleasure. I have no idea what pleasure is . . . well, that's not exactly true, my daughter gives me pleasure; what happiness I ever knew she gave me. . . .

I struggle with hate and despair; I hated what people did to me; but there was no rescue, no comfort . . . just pain. . . . When the little girl in me comes out, she brings pain. . . . I guess that's true with my other personalities . . . at least that's what Dr. V. [her therapist] tells me. . . . I don't know if I'm multiple or not. I think I am; I have periods where I don't remember anything, and people tell me I'm being nasty and angry; or I may sit in the corner and whimper for hours and not remember anything. I may, every once in a while, hear a voice in my head; but I don't have long conversations with my other personalities like Molly or Beth . . . I'm not like them . . . I find myself in the past a lot . . . it tires me . . . look at me . . . do you like what you see? . . . I just want to die and disappear from the earth. . . .

Halloween Night: Satan's Dance

Nora described her terror as Halloween approached:

Even earlier in the week, I found myself panicking . . . it [moving back to the past] was going to happen all over again. . . . I asked staff to strap me into the "geri" chair [a special chair with leather restraints for arms and legs] beginning at eight and to let me out at twelve. By then, the worst would have passed, and I would be safe. I wanted Mary and Jim [staff members] to sit with me . . . I needed help through this.

It began right before eight . . . just after they strapped me into the chair . . . I started to lose it . . . I was back . . . there . . . that place . . . the empty field filled with men in Halloween suits and clowns running around with blood smeared on their faces, and white chalk around their eyes and mouths.

And then one clown, I'll never forget him . . . dressed in a black cape, and black pants . . . his entire face covered with a white paste. . . . Purple lines came down from his forehead and beside his ears, all intersecting at his mouth. When he smiled at me, it looked like a band of strings pulling back his features, against the white background. It was terrible; his face turned into a mass of cuts and scars, stretching out toward his skull . . . he wore a peaked hat made out of leather and bird feathers. He grabbed my arm and dragged me to a huge boulder, sitting in the center of a clearing. Beyond the trees . . . blackness. . . . Torches lit the circle.

On the boulder, a young girl had been laid out; she must have been fifteen, sixteen . . . her body, stretched, seemed lifeless . . . two men held her down: one, her hands, the other her feet; another two clowns, with smaller hats than the clown holding me, came up . . . each held two blocks of wood. . . . Two blocks were placed under her hands and feet . . . the men placed her so each hand and foot lay on top of a block of wood . . . they kept her down. And then the clown man holding me came up to her . . . I don't remember what he said . . . some kind of chant . . . I hear it now as a raving . . . a torrent of words . . . he shoved a scarf into the girl's mouth . . . and started massaging her body . . . the crowd chanting . . . he pulled me up to the stone, so I stood directly opposite the girl . . . it was cold . . . I was naked . . . so was she [Nora at this point is shivering uncontrollably].

The clown man motioned to someone in the circle; a woman dressed in what looked like black leotards, with wide red lines painted down the front and back, handed him a mallet and four huge wooden nails . . . the girl just lay there, silent, eyes staring up at the black sky . . . she had obviously been drugged, since she hadn't moved during all of this. . . . The crowd, around the perim-

eter of a circle, began singing, chanting, words mixed with shrieks
. . . the clown man walked around the boulder, muttering, holding
the mallet and nails above his head, imploring Satan for guidance
. . . Suddenly the clown screamed at the crowd for silence . . . you
could hear a pin drop . . . it was so quiet . . . just the wind made
any sound.

The clown man said a prayer to the Devil . . . then he took the
mallet and one of the nails and drove it through the girl's hand,
into the block of wood underneath. . . . He did it again with the
other hand, and then with her feet. She screamed once and then . . .
nothing. . . . I guess she passed out . . . the clown smiled at me . . .
kissed me on the lips . . . then took me by the hand and put a
knife into it . . . you can't imagine how cold it was . . . I could
barely feel my feet . . . he led me to the boulder, guided my hand
with the knife in it, down one of her legs. . . . Her flesh opened
up. . . . I'll never forget it . . . that pinkness and then my hand,
the knife covered with blood . . . blood running down her leg. . . .
I cut her other leg . . . more bleeding . . . it wouldn't stop. . . .

The clown put a cup underneath her thigh . . . he collected some
blood and made me drink it . . . it was so heavy . . . thick . . .
[Nora is gagging through this description] I got so sick . . . vomiting all over the place. . . . The clown put a pill in my mouth and
made me drink more blood . . . the nausea disappeared, and I just
stood there, watching clown man smear her blood all over her
body . . . I was so cold. . . . The next thing I knew someone from
the circle picked me up, put a cape over my shoulders and carried
me back to the circle's edge . . . she wiped the blood off my face
and gave me something sweet to drink. . . .

The clown man made a speech saying we had to appease the
great god; how this was a blood sacrifice, a sign of our devotion to
Satan, an offering to the triumph of Evil. . . . he turned away from
the boulder, kneeled down and put his hands on the ground; but
then he jumped up and screamed something, I don't remember
what, at the sky . . . the woman in the black leotard stepped out
again from the circle and handed him a lighted torch . . . he moved
back toward the girl . . . again, another prayer, this time a high
pitch to his voice . . . everyone in the circle began to sway and
moan, some people moved even further into the forest, chanting a
prayer I could not understand . . . the clown man started spinning

with the torch saying vicious things about God and praising Satan
and crying for the victory of evil . . . tears streaming down his face
. . . then suddenly he stopped spinning, took the torch and held it
to the girl's stomach . . . it was horrible! . . . the stench . . . the
smell of burning flesh. He yelled again . . . "The glory of Satan;
praise be the glory of Satan" . . . and took the torch . . . holding it
over the girl's face . . . the sound of the burning . . . and the smell
. . . flesh turning into rivers of fat . . . and . . . then . . . just
charred skin . . . terrible! . . . terrible! . . .

Nora looks up at me. She pauses for a long time; her eyes seem
to be staring far off into the distance.

For a week before Halloween I couldn't eat because cooked food
smelled like burning flesh, and any drink, anything in a cup or
glass reminded me of raw human blood . . . it was days before I
could put anything into my mouth.

I remember around nine or ten, some of the kids from Chapman
building [the adolescent ward] came over; they were all dressed in
clown outfits but there was a huge fat man, probably one of the
staff, dressed like a clown . . . in black, with white chalk over his
face. . . . Jim told me when I saw him I started vomiting and
screaming . . . my eyeballs rolled up into my head; and I passed
out for a few minutes. . . .

But it wasn't over yet . . . the ceremony, I mean, in the forest . . .
after the clown man finished . . . the torch . . . burning her . . .
she was beyond recognition . . . her body . . . a mass of . . . it's
just too horrible to speak about. . . . I couldn't look . . . her body
was rolled up into some kind of blanket with marks of Satan all
over it . . . and they carried her off . . . clown man kneeled and
whispered a prayer to Satan . . . I couldn't hear him . . . then he
turned to me, and ripped the cape off my shoulders, grabbed me
by the arms and threw me onto the ground. I lay there for a long,
long time . . . being raped by him, repeatedly, and others in the
circle . . . the rest watched . . . silently, no words . . . just the
noise of breathing . . . and the movement of clothes . . . and the
pushing into me until it hurt so much I felt I was about to be split
open . . . I blacked out . . . or I went to another place . . . maybe
another personality formed . . . I don't know.

After they finished, clown man motioned to the crowd to move in closer . . . they chanted the words . . . "not to tell, not to tell . . . silence . . . silence . . ." and then in the name of Satan, clown man threatened I would die if I ever told. . . . After that I was given something to drink . . . the next thing I remember is waking up in my room, the following morning, cleaned up, with bandages on me, but very, very sore. Every orifice of my body ached. . . . I had bruises around my genitals . . . I could barely move. . . .

After they took me out of the geri chair, I vowed I would slit my wrists in a warm bathtub and watch myself die. . . . I couldn't stop crying . . . it had been an awful night. . . . Jim and Mary carried me to my room . . . they changed my clothes and gave me a little water to sip. I kept thinking how much fun it would be to be a little girl doing cartwheels across the hall . . . or maybe I could slip through a crack in the window and escape the hospital and find some quiet place in the woods to die.

That night, with the help of major tranquilizers, Nora slept, free of what she called her "voodoo ritual of hallucination," which now lay bounded within the protected confines of the hospital. She could find some peace because she was safe from retribution if she revealed secrets. And she had "told."

The terror wrought by the clown man dissipated, and in the morning Nora was left with the coldness of her memories, the horror of the world tormenting her consciousness, and the certain knowledge that if she left the hospital she would die. I asked Nora if she were sure that she wanted her story told; she assured me that if the cult wanted her, if they were really bent on kidnaping her, nothing could protect her, but that she would kill to protect her daughter from the cult.

The Will to Die as Reflection on Life

How believable are Nora's experiences? From what I saw, believable. Even if embellished, Nora's narrative possessed a truth content written not only in her body but in the stream of the narrative itself. Nora had too firm a grasp of consensual reality to be delusional or even playing at living in horror; the human self is simply not capable of acting out these terrors on the body without some compelling reason. To call Nora masochistic would be completely to undermine the truth content of her narrative. To attribute a delusional madness to her speech would be inconsistent with other aspects of her persona and her grasp of shared realities.

Listening to her language, watching her face, witnessing the injuries to her body, one would conclude that Nora fought some terrible presence inside her, memories that took her not to delusion but to a real place: abreaction as truth. That much I am convinced of. If the body can be understood as a text, the world that surrounded Nora was defined by death—a body torn apart, violated, penetrated, locked away, a body defined by genitals pierced with pins, burning fluids forced into her orifices, ears burned with matches, excrement smeared over her face, a body whose reality existed as an instrument for the will of others. Is it any wonder that Nora lives in a world defined by its fatalism and the struggle to kill oneself?

Indeed, Nora may be crazy; maybe what I heard is a massive delusion, built up over years of self-preoccupation as she journeyed inward to try to explain and make sense out of the abusive horrors she experienced. Whether or not the specifics are historically true, however, is not the issue or the point. What is the point and what is true are the reflections Nora carries within and the bruises, scars, and injuries embodied in the very immanence of her physical being. That is the truth of Nora's being. *It is written in her body.*[3]

To be in life as the victim of blood rituals, to witness ritual sacrifices, to be raped publicly, given drugs, forced to drink human blood, to have been raped as a child, as a teenager—to be in life in this way is to live life as if it were a chase after death. How does one make sense out of the human commitment to live life as if its objective were death? That is the stark reality of Nora's universe and, to a lesser extent, Kimberly's. Both found themselves at different times desiring death to wipe out intolerable forms of emotional and psychological pain. Their multiplicity is an effort to deal not only with the effects of trauma and abuse, horrible enough, but with the ever-present drive to die.

[3]Compare with Cixous: "*Voice-cry*. Agony—the spoken 'word' exploded, blown to bits by suffering and anger" (Cixous and Clément 1986: 94). Or with Kristeva: "Thus the truth of the signifer, namely, its separability, otherness, death, can be seen to be exerted on the flesh itself—as on words" (1986a: 236).

For those of us interested in what this experience means as commentary on evil, power, domination, and patriarchy, the answers are equally as bleak and despairing. Nora survives; Nora survives her abreactions; she survives the grim facts of her life; she deals with divorce and divorce lawyers, with a family that has essentially denied her existence and repudiated her being. She lives in a world without connection and friends, but she manages on occasion some humor and will (or tenacity), particularly in relation to protecting her daughter. But despair and fatalism inevitably poison whatever will to life Nora manages to express. It is remarkable that Nora has remained alive as long as she has.

That Nora's suicide attempts have always been in the hospital testifies to an element of life, something of a will to live. On her few sign-outs, she has not thrown herself into Baltimore's Inner Harbor or jumped off a building. The brutal encounters in the fields, the ritual dismemberments, the torn bodies, the threats from cult members and rapists—to live after that, to marry and attempt a "conventional" life, suggests that fighting against the will to die (which Nora sees as the will of the world *in relation to her*) suggests an equally compelling, if not equally powerful, opposition, a will to life which may be testimonial to Freud's Eros in its greatest sense.

It is also testimony to the power of language, both to embody the experience in feeling and image and to provide bridges back to memories that haunt the self as pain and torture. Abreacting such experiences through feelings released by flashback (and being able to sustain the abreaction through the holding efforts of others, in these cases the hospital staff) is central to the self's movement toward a consolidation and to some semblance of possibility and normality in a world not defined by cruelty and death. In these contexts normality is not to be avoided, as it is for the postmodernists.

Further, these women are enmeshed in a multiplicity of identities that derive from widely different developmental "moments"; it is therefore impossible to say that Kimberly or Nora possesses a self whose core rests on a progressive consolidation of identifications specific to any developmental stage. No single developmental moment has been superseded, because both women find themselves occupied by "personalities" whose age is constant and invariable. Kimberly exists as a five-year-old, an eight-year-old, a fifteen-year-old, a twenty-year-old, and so on. Boundaries, if any, between self and other are totally dependent on which personality happens to be "out." These dissociated and fractured psychological worlds, totally defined by brutal physical and sexual abuse, are akin to the Hobbesian terror of the natural condition; therefore what is inside the self provides no relief. There is no place in the world where the self may withdraw and feel safe. Only "rescuer" alters provide any distance from the experience itself. What defines both "inside" and "outside" is the memory of terror and the immanence and presence of the feeling of terror in the form of multiple and separable personalities. Those qualities that keep the self together—what Hobbes calls "reckoning" and Kant "reason"—possess almost no function, and terror, horror, or rage calls forth or brings out the differing selves.

Conclusion: A Self without Boundaries

The presence of multiplicity in Kimberly and Nora, a product of ongoing and traumatic sexual and physical abuse, promises not a spontaneity of soul, a freedom or liberation wiping away decadent histories, but just the opposite: oppression, domination, and denial of being. Women with multiple personalities demonstrate not the power of critical reason in deconstructing moribund modern environments (of thought and practice) but the consequence, the terror, of actually living out an existential process based on multiplicity. Their words testify to how unfree a self without an identity in time can be, how dangerous is the reality of an unmoored self, the Baudrillardian notion of a self without boundaries.

Such women who have firsthand knowledge of fractured consciousness scream out for a world that might lead them toward a unitary conception of who they are as persons, identities rooted in continuities, traditions, and histories. To be free in the world, one must possess an identity capable of defining what the world is and capable of understanding itself as the end result of historical development. Postmodernists have neglected the importance of the psychological function of boundary and of the role of historical connection in forging self-knowledge. They mistakenly confuse what a core self "is" with the lack of freedom to reject the past, convention, normality, and so on. But it is precisely the resilience of a core self, a strong sense of one's unitary being, that allows such "freedom" to proceed in creative and nondestructive forms. It is the lack of a core self, an identity that could successfully navigate the journey from primitive symbolization to complex social interaction, which brings to multiple personalities not freedom but enslavement within the chaotic conditions of an unstable multiplicity. Such enslavement, I argue, haunts any human being, multiple personality or not, who lives and exists in the world without a core conception of self.

Not all convention, history, causality, and belief are debilitating to identity creation. Although there is much to say for taking a fresh look at what modernity creates and offers, there are equally compelling reasons for retaining certain modernist assumptions, in this case certain psychoanalytic notions: that a stable subjectivity is essential; that the self's identity needs to be rooted in a firm sense of boundary distinction; that identity carries with it certain assumptions about sexuality, gender, and preoedipal emotional experience; that family and history work on both conscious and unconscious strata of the self; and that unconscious or split-off forms of psychological "reality" affect, often drastically, whatever we discover and internalize along the way. Kimberly and Nora so powerfully demonstrate the tragedy of living without a fixed sense of identity: their multiplicity condemns them from its rootedness in brutality and terror.

Finally, their experiences, like Molly's, are sad examples of the perversion of power and the arrogance of patriarchal assumptions over the possession of women. Certainly this kind of sadism and power, used to inflict harm, possesses radically sexist, misogynist dimensions. But to the extent that power moves beyond its ordered field and beyond its respect for the lives and bodies of others, to the extent that power becomes embodied in ritualistic and horribly sadistic practices, to the extent power becomes an excuse to draw life from others without giving life back—to that extent, what these cults have practiced on Nora and Kimberly is not much different from political forms of power which define sovereignty as the infliction of harm, the punishment of bodies, and the depletion of life.

That such objectives are found in the political spaces of the twentieth century, if not in all histories that contain stories about the exercise of power, should not be surprising. Power, however, is not some disembodied force that suddenly appears; it is an extension, if not a projection, of what is collectively human. Values and practices created by human beings produce power; but when power becomes abusive, it is the human community, the collective patterns of nature and human nature, which bears the responsibility for not only the creation of that power but for its transgressions. The sadistic patterns that pass for everyday life and the glorification of destructiveness that motivates so much of modern politics—which itself are products of our world—find themselves grotesquely magnified in the narratives of these women. What happened to Nora and Kimberly, what happens when nations, states, and groups find themselves raped, overrun, and decimated, are grim reminders that power, as a demonstration of human will, possesses a face whose ugliness has the power to turn us all into stone and cinders.

7   PLACELESSNESS AND ASYLUM

The consciousness of the person with multiple personalities is excluded from the most fundamental ontological position of human life: knowledge of self and place as a continuous presence within identifiable forms of historical experience. To discover a sense of place is to begin the recovery of one's "identifiable presence" in a continuing history. Yet the tragedy for the multiple personality is the inhospitality of society to this kind of quest. Where are such persons to go? What is to be the fate of those human beings who face the terror of these disorienting forms of psychological placelessness?

The antipsychiatry literature of postmodernism has made a blanket indictment of all forms of asylum. Yet asylum may offer refuge from the alienating processes of power dependent on a civil society that often intensifies and exacerbates psychological disconnection. Is there a problem with a concept of asylum or with the way power embodied in institutions degenerates into repressive structure and transforms asylum into imprisonment?

Both schizophrenics and multiple personalities suffer from radical forms of psychological disconnection. It seems reasonable to think about a theory of refuge which confronts the foundations of such disconnection, particularly its origins in the self *and* in the effects of the power that has unhinged consciousness.

If one grants René Girard's (1986) view that the victim as scapegoat participates in a kind of mirror relationship with the surrounding society, that the victim produces forms of social pain, asylum may provide these "outcasts" with protection from a madness that arises in the structure of community itself. This is certainly the case for the multiple personality.

Modern communitarian theorists have failed to acknowledge that the community and its interrelated forms of power may provoke a madness that persecutes members who, for whatever reason, find themselves vulnerable to the psychological action of scapegoating. Girard suggests that society has a need to construct an Other who persecutes (the scapegoat); community in this respect becomes oppressive, thus its intolerance to forms of psychological dislocation which appear disorienting and confusing. "Those who make up the crowd are always potential persecutors, for they dream of purging the community of the impure elements that corrupt it, the traitors who undermine it" (16). The community projects categories of otherness to be circumscribed by power and repressed by the institutions supporting power. Thus a political and moral objective is intensified by the self's very real psychological alienation. "The community must effectively be emptied of its poisons. It must feel liberated and reconciled within itself. This is implied in the conclusion of most myths" (92). The creation of outcasts derives from the community's need to embody in the Other what it fears most in itself. The community requires the exclusion of difference, its banishment or containment from public view. The effect appears in the creation of scapegoats, others that can be considered less than human. "The perpetual conjunction in myths of a very guilty victim with a conclusion that is both violent and liberating can only be explained by the extreme force of the scapegoat mechanism" (42).

The scapegoating process traps persons who find themselves "seeing" and "perceiving" the world in forms radically different from those of the collective or group. The effect on the schizophrenic is more obvious in this regard than it is on the multiple personality, although multiple personalities often find themselves excluded from families and relationships because of the abruptness of shifting or the bizarre quality of whatever personality happens to be in view. The "madness" of scapegoating lies not only in the pain it brings to the victim but in the process of exclusion it enforces: to be a scapegoat is to find oneself alone, outside, beyond protected forms of civil life. It is to be uncontained and therefore lost or terrorized. Yet scapegoating also serves to blind the community to its own culpability, its own failure to take responsibility for creating out of its own fabric a category of otherness which denies, and sometimes defiles, critical forms of human agency.

Girard's analysis of myth, like Wilfred Bion's (1959) psychoanalytic study of group action, forcefully demonstrates that madness possesses a group dimension, that the desire to hurt, to inflict pain, inheres in the collective, its agents, and its moral positions— whether that persecutory dimension lies in a cult, a social group, or the larger collective or nation itself.

The Antipsychiatric Critique:
On Not Listening to Madness

I turn for a moment, before elaborating in somewhat more detail on an approach to asylum, to the antipsychiatry critique of postmodernism, especially Foucault's argument in *Madness and Civilization*, which has some disturbing implications that arise from his position on moral judgment and the status of the disconnected self.

In Foucault's reading, madness in the nineteenth century found itself "imprisoned in a moral world"; constraint was enforced by "guilt and judgment," and the physician changed from jailer into the "wise man . . . Father and Judge, Family and Law" (1965: 267– 72). Judgment, and its social correlates, replaced the use of chains and dungeons: "Everything was organized so that the madman would recognize himself in a world of judgment that enveloped him on all sides; he must know that he is watched, judged and condemned; from transgression to punishment, the connection must be evident, as a guilt recognized by all" (267).

Foucault's strongest argument, however, lies in his condemnation of the asylum as a form of imprisonment and confinement, as an institution of moral discipline: "But the asylum, in this community of madmen, placed the mirrors in such a way that the madman, when all was said and done, inevitably surprised himself, despite himself, *as a madman*. Freed from chains that made it a purely observed object, madness lost, paradoxically, the essence of its liberty, which was solitary exaltation. . . . it was finally chained to the humiliation of being its own object" (264–65).

I do not completely reject his argument: institutions, moral norms, prevailing discourses, do affect how mental illness is perceived, how it is treated and, most important, how the community chooses to manage through its practices those individuals whose speech, action, and internal epistemologies move against the prevailing consensus. My central criticism of his position lies in the absence of empathy for the person, a silence on how to heal or at least ameliorate intense physical and psychological pain.

A book and argument that has caused more recent notoriety is Deleuze and Guattari's *Anti-Oedipus*, widely quoted as a manifesto of the postmodernist hostility even to the idea of "mental illness," much less to any theory of asylum. Its argument is consistent with, for example, Baudrillard and Lyotard's critique of capitalism as a manifestation of the insatiability of desire in a materialism dominated by modernist structures of production and authority. It is certainly not consistent with, for example, Kristeva's view of the suffering that accompanies mental illness and the fall into emptiness and Irigaray's account of the victimization imposed on women by an exchange culture. Both Irigaray and Kristeva affirm the importance of healing, seeing in psychoanalytic perspectives an effort to ameliorate pain. Not so for the postmodernists: the purpose of theory is to unmask all forms of healing, which are in effect social practices designed to enforce a regime of power on the self.

For Deleuze and Guattari, psychoanalysis, Freud's oedipal theory, the treatment of psychosis in hospitals, judgments about illness—all are manifestations of a corrupt modernity that produces excludable human beings as efficiently as it does commodities. Without the context of the crazy desiring patterns of capitalism and its moral ideologies, oedipal theory would make no sense; psychoanalysis would be ineffective as a mode of power dominating perception and desire; and mental hospitals would be unnecessary. Economic transformation in the relations of production, new postcapitalist attitudes toward desire, and the elimination of epistemes governing the practices of the psychological sciences will transform the conditions and interpretive codes of the self. Old meanings will be discarded; new languages discovered; and, most important, interpretation will be "liberated" from its indebtedness to psychoanalysis and oedipal theory.

In the place of psychoanalysis, Deleuze and Guattari would have "schizo-analysis," a kind of linguistic logic that transforms perception of what madness "is"; the mad would no longer be seen as sick but as laudable examples of rebellion against the epistemes of modern society.

— Deleuze and Guattari offer a clarion call to psychological and political revolution; the agents will be the schizophrenic, the mad, the psychically displaced. "Why does [society] confine its madmen and madwomen instead of seeing in them its own heroes and heroines, its own fulfillment?" (1977: 245). They require a "decoding" that blasts away the "nondecomposable blocks" of meaning which keep the self riveted in capitalist "schizo-flows." This process opens up cracks in experience; schizo-analysis erodes the moribund meaning structure of modernism; it reveals, in Lyotard's words, those "intermundia that perhaps are visible only to children, madmen and primitives" (1989: 243).

Capitalism, and its "privatization," effectively represses and even attempts to destroy a kind of "primitive" consciousness which seeks to move beyond ideological formulation, and what Deleuze and Guattari call the "territorialization" of desire. Systems of production, "organs of 'private man,' . . . the abstraction of monetary quantities" (244–45), impose on the self a "yoke of despotism whose effect is castration" (112).

Deleuze and Guattari argue for a psychological "breakthrough" that will dehistoricize consciousness, that will cast off linguistic, ethical, and interpretive "despotisms" as well as supportive political structures. Theirs is an effort to escape not only all categorization but all sense of inherited or traditional value. The power of "schizo-analysis," then, lies in its deconstructive logic: it "de-territorializes"; it breaks up the family (destruction of the daddy-mommy-me triad); it affirms atheism (annihilation of beliefs that derive from the Judeo-Christian tradition). Schizo-analysis advocates nomads or nomadism, selves free from habits, claims to specific territories, and rootedness in any sense of unity or essence. To free oneself of family, belief, and structure—the governing *territories* of capitalism—is to become truly multiple; it is to be schizophrenic in Deleuze and Guattari's political use of this term.

The psychotic, in their view, is actually free, because psychosis releases the self from connection to and dependence on the normalizing society. (Compare this view with, for example, Kristeva's [1986a] dismal account of the debilitating effects of the "true/real," the self's psychotic space.) Or, in the words of the editor of the volume: "The first task of the revolutionary . . . is to learn from the psychotic how to shake off the Oedipal yoke and the effects of power, in order to initiate a radical politics of desire freed from all beliefs" (xxi). Quite a project! "Schizo-analysis" is the method of this liberation. Or, to put it another way: to see the world as the schizophrenic does is to liberate the self from the moral and psychological despotisms of the modernist period.

Or, as Foucault describes Deleuze and Guattari's project in his Preface to *Anti-Oedipus*: "Withdraw allegiance from the old categories of the Negative (law, limit, castration, lack, lacuna) which Western thought has so long held sacred as a form of power and an access to reality. Prefer what is positive and multiple, difference over uniformity, flows over unities, mobile arrangements over systems. Believe that what is productive is not sedentary but nomadic" (Deleuze and Guattari 1977: xiii). Nomadic in what sense? To be psychically or emotionally nomadic, without going crazy, one needs a strong ego structure—precisely the kind of internalized unity which Foucault, postmodernism, and Lacan generally attack. Further, Foucault writes, Deleuze and Guattari criticize what they see as the central psychological enforcers of modernism: "The poor technicians of desire—psychoanalysts and semiologists of every sign and symptom—who would subjugate the multiplicity of desire to the twofold law of structure and lack" (xii–xiii). In his Preface, Foucault calls *Anti-Oedipus* a great book of ethics. But, as I see it, Deleuze and Guattari are attacking even the possibility of an ethics or an ethics conceived as a response to human suffering and alienation. If anything, Deleuze and Guattari hold views consistent with Baudrillard's radical critique of ethics, his dismissal of the idea of coherence and identity, his embracing of the nihilist concept of the "excrescence of meaning" and the notion that modernity has rendered corrupt and useless all theories of meaning and empathy.

If Deleuze and Guattari are extolling the schizoid experiences of detachment and objectification as a source of political revelation, then their argument demonstrates an enormous insensitivity to what this pain, this "schizophrenia," creates in human beings. As E. Victor Wolfenstein writes about their project: "If they were concerned with actual schizophrenic experience, then *Anti-Oedipus* might have been compassionate rather than celebratory [of fragmentation and breakup]. As it is, we are treated to schizophrenia-as-spectacle, an enjoyable pastime for those who relish cruelty. . . . Breaking with the philosophy of identity is more difficult than it might seem" (forthcoming). (In *Portrait of Dora*, Cixous pays a great deal more attention to the suffering of the hysteric than Deleuze and Guattari do to the suffering of the schizophrenic. The pain of *living* schizophrenia is completely absent in their analysis. The pain of *living* hysteria stands out in both Cixous's psychological awareness and Clément's historical interpretation of specific feminine behaviors—notably sorcery—that paternal power saw as deviant or abnormal.)

Schizophrenics, of course, are much different from multiple personalities; in schizophrenia the issue is not separable and distinct personalities but fragments of self-experience embedded in delusional projections that function as self-limiting epistemologies. To be schizophrenic is to be without "personality" or persona; it is to live outside the knowledge frames of consensual reality. In addition, the schizophrenic substitutes internally derived, delusional symbologies for existing and embodied others (Glass 1987).

To be a multiple personality is to have those personas; it is to live and be with others. The profound disconnection lies in the lack of relationship between personalities who have no awareness of another's existence. Theirs is a different kind of disconnection than the schizophrenic's; each personality lives in an existing present without constructing delusional symbologies. To be multiple is not necessarily to be delusional, but nonetheless it is a peculiar kind of madness, in the sense that possessing several distinct personalities, each with its own history and date of birth, is to exist in a psychological world of enormous dislocation and pain.

For Deleuze and Guattari, the schizophrenic's linguistic self signifies the act of liberation: the breaking up of signifiers, the dislocation of language and therefore of meaning—which more accurately corresponds to the flows of desire in a postmodern, hyperreal world. For Foucault, madness received its highest expression in its "solitary exaltation," the self living in the midst of its delusional terror, without the moral constraint of convention. Deleuze and Guattari take this argument one step further: schizophrenia breaks up or fragments social and moral experience; this disintegration or "deconstruction" is the precondition for political revolution. To be schizophrenic, then, is not only to be free of society's confining meaning— its texts, its moral codes, and its practices—it is also to be liberated from psychologically defined *territories* such as the oedipal theory which force consciousness to conform to prevailing ideologies. It is a freedom in their view celebrating the fragmentation of experience, the destruction of meaning, and the liberation of desire from the productive needs of capitalism.

But what kind of freedom is implied by equating multiplicity with the pursuit of fragmentation? What, for example, do schizophrenics tell us about the worlds they inhabit; what is the effect of their "multiplicity"; what kinds of "truths" lie in these worlds? Does it make sense to speak of delusion as a form of freedom, liberation?

What kind of freedom does Chuck experience when he "knows" that his body is being ground up into sausage to be stuffed into casings made by local police; what does Dana know about the nature of desire when she finds herself living in the belly of a huge whale, sloshing back and forth, constantly sick to her stomach, thinking that the whale's digestive acid, in the form of moisture in the air, eats away at her skin. Should such persons be left in their delusional "places"? Should their terror be glorified as an example of a kind of revolutionary praxis? What Foucault speaks of as the Great Fear in the mid-eighteenth century, the fear of the madman, is also reflected in what the *madman* fears. Why chain people to that kind of knowledge system? In the name of their liberty? This is an issue— what does liberty mean from the standpoint of the delusional or mad self?—that Thomas Szasz never confronts in *The Myth of Mental Illness* (1961).

Deleuze and Guattari take the utterances of the mad—their texts, the literal form of their words—as insight. Further, they equate the expressiveness of madness with the imagery or symbology of the limit-breaking artist. (Kristeva refuses to fall into this trap.) And given their fascination with expressionist art and literature, they invest madness with poetic and revolutionary dimensions. Nietzsche, Antoinin Artaud, Henry Miller, Beckett, William Burroughs use words to describe states of being that move in much different directions than do capitalism and materialism. But the words are those of the artists; the letters possess a structure, context, and clarity precisely because these letters and images contain meaning. Art extends meaning; it transcends conventional perceptions; it reveals breakthroughs; it deconstructs. Yet the utterances of the madman are not organized; not only do they lack a transcendent point of view, but the words or "notes" of madness find themselves garbled, like several voices coming over the same telephone receiver. It is a cacophony of sound—letters, gathering together as words, without an underlying coherence that allows for communication. How can a noncommunicative linguistic posture be considered revolutionary? The answer escapes me.

Persons who sit for hours without uttering a word or who walk in circles lest they step out of them and be killed, who fear drinking water from a fountain because it contains acid or who hear voices commanding them from outer space, or who, like Kimberly, house several personalities in the head: what is the meaning to this kind of isolation? Where is the "schizo-flow" in the texts of these human beings? Further, so much of madness, particularly schizophrenia, is nonverbal: a distortion of body and muscle, a radical caricature of appearances written into the flesh itself. Where are the messages or signs in these kinds of behaviors? Where in distorted musculature, gross variations in weight, is the revelation, the artistic construction?

To be an artist is a way of life; to be a schizophrenic and not to be an artist is to be shuffled out of society, a living human tragedy. Most insanity is mundane and silent; it lacks a communicative dimension, and even to embody it in language, to understand one sentence out of a thousand, may be a triumph. Even to utter a sentence may signify a therapeutic breakthrough. I find it ironic that Deleuze and Guattari, so sensitive to the "text," to its authority, should find as heroes those human beings for whom texts are often garbled collections of words or who refuse to embody their presence in the world in any kind of linguistic text.

There are moments in *Madness and Civilization* when it appears that Foucault would rather leave the mad in the midst of their ravings. Why rescue them, he seems to be saying, when the effect of that rescue is to contain madness in moral injunctions that imprison consciousness? Yet, when Chuck observes that "pain is the name of the game" and that the only way to stop the pain is to slice off his head, one wonders about the justice of this kind of solitary existence. In Foucault's view, the "asylum must represent the great continuity of social morality. The values of family and work, all the acknowledged virtues now [during the period of moral treatment early in the nineteenth century] reign in the asylum" (1965: 257). I have been struck, however, by how often patients, including women with multiple personalities, speak of family and work as desired objectives; how social relationships—the competence of good work, fair treatment at a job, intimate connections with family and friends, the presence of caring—become the governing conditions of what *they* perceive to be the decent and good life.

Several factors, in addition to the economic contradictions Deleuze and Guattari describe, prevent these social pleasures and competencies from being realized. For example, a great deal of literature suggests that biological, chemical, and genetic factors may be contributory to schizophrenia; Deleuze and Guattari simply ignore such research. They do not consider psychodynamic factors, such as splitting, unconscious fantasy, and projective identification, the role of skewed communication patterns in the family, the very real problems of boundary and object constancy: all these causative factors are dismissed as concepts belonging to a superstructure supportive of a corrupt modernity/capitalism.

Foucault, Szasz, and Deleuze and Guattari construct effective arguments against psychiatry as a regime of domination, a "practice" whose epistemes reinforce the modern human sciences and their obsession with control. That, however, is one side of the issue. It is one thing to raise questions about a theory of practice; it is an entirely different matter to glorify a state of mind which has left millions debilitated and useless.

For the schizophrenic, consciousness finds itself plagued with the wish to die, with waking nightmares and delusional terrors that Michael Eigen describes as "fragmentation . . . bits and pieces of meaning and meaninglessness, chaotic blankness, dry periods, and psychic dust storms" (1986: 136), just the sort of phenomena post-modernists idealize. To see these post-Nietzschean disconnections actually being embodied or represented not just in text but in the suffering of real human beings places the nihilist argument of De-leuze and Guattari in a context that raises serious questions about how to use, in an ideological sense, human suffering. Human be-ings suffer; letters do not. It is not enough to dismiss what Kristeva calls "the suffering of emptiness" (1986b: 258), the schizophrenic's "disavowal of reality . . . explosion of identity" (226, 235), the "(psy-chotic) hole in which the subject might be lost" (1986a: 230) by say-ing these perceptions or delusions derive from the production of desire and its inhibition or from socially imposed categories distin-guishing between reason and unreason. Madness, either as psy-chosis or in its peculiar nonpsychotic form in women with multiple personalities, places the self in discernible pain.

Asylum as Confinement

It is by now commonplace that warehouses for the insane, bru-talizing institutions that enforce normality, inhibit effective treat-ment for psychosis. That part of the critique of institutionalization, which began with Erving Goffman's analysis in *Asylums* (1961), has been absorbed into much of the theoretical landscape. It has also had a great deal to do with the social movement advocating the clos-ing down of mental hospitals and the use of medications to treat chronic patients on an out-patient basis, a movement that has pro-duced large numbers of homeless who for the most part exhibit psy-chotic symptoms. The psychically homeless, whether in hospitals or on the streets, suffer from enormous deprivation and pose serious social problems. An acknowledgement of this deprivation, some sensitivity to it, seems strangely absent in Deleuze and Guattari's polemic. Sherry Turkle notes this absence: "Although [anti-psychia-try in France] attacks mythologies of 'normality,' it substitutes myth-ologies of deviancy of the excluded, of revolutionaries, gangsters, and psychotics, all 'outside of the law' of capitalist society. . . . Nos-talgia and romanticism may be keeping the French anti-psychiatric movement lively, but may also be undercutting its productivity as a meaningful political struggle . . . idealizing the 'pure' (i.e., unmedicated) state of madness may make good poetry, but it may be bad for the patient" (1980: 177, 179).

Perhaps the plight and the tragedy of the mad might be described in the context of Ludwig Wittgenstein's observation of the "bewitchment of our intelligence by means of language" (1953: 47). Language encloses the perceptual world; it keeps consciousness riveted to the specific terms or symbols in any discourse. The schizophrenic, then, in Wittgenstein's terms experiences a form of linguistic entrapment; text and self merge. "A *picture* held us captive. And we could not get outside it, for it lay in our language and language seemed to repeat it to us inexorably" (48). Kristeva makes a similar observation: "Psychotic discourse forecloses reality" (1986a: 232). Similarly with the multiple personality: it is impossible to step outside the relation established between language and identity: the linguistic picture becomes the self, in whatever alter-form.

Foucault's postmodernist critique understands power "as the multiplicity of force relations immanent in the sphere in which they operate and which constitute their own organization" (1976: 92). Such a description captures the confining aspects of such institutions as mental hospitals, schools, and prisons; these places impose power; they coerce. The issue is not that power coerces or that institutions may radically alienate the self from justice; the postmodernists and psychoanalytic feminists agree on these points. What is left out of the postmodernist critique of power and the celebration of multiplicity is the person who endures not only the presence of the institution, which may or may not be sympathetic, but the chaotic, internal currents of delusion, hallucination, terror, and victimization.

To hear persecuting, sadistic messages is more than an instance of a corrupt society or its agents of power "implanting" voices in the self or, in Deleuze and Guattari's terms, externalizing Oedipus "in the symbolic order, in the institutional order, in the community order, the sectorial order" (1979: 359). It is, rather, a complex interplay, a dialectic, between inner and outer, between the hidden world of fantasy and terror, the split-off self, undeniable biological factors in the case of schizophrenia, and the fear of having to confront the normal world. That "voice" cannot be expunged by rearranging institutions; its presence requires a listening, a sensitivity literally to the "soul" of the self. It is not enough to argue that to wake up the self (Deleuze and Guattari's position) requires a political blast against the institutions of power. Power and its perversion undoubtedly play a role in dislocating self, especially in multiple personality disorders; yet there are certain psychodynamic and physiological factors—for example, self-hypnosis in the case of multiple personality—which contribute greatly to states of mind which run counter to the governing consensus.

Turkle highlights problems in the postmodernist position when she observes, "The tragedy of the psychotic is the tragedy of our impotence and our ignorance of better solutions" to the dislocations of mental illness (1980: 175). Yet even Turkle succumbs occasionally to valorizing the psychotic, to seeing the psychotic as a political radical or social outcast who nevertheless is able to stake out a claim. The disintegration of state power, she argues, produces victims (scapegoats; her argument is similar to Girard's) who possess a shared reality and a natural alliance: "In advanced industrial capitalism, the community that was once represented by the state is in dissolution. Citizens are no longer in what used to be the 'normal' relationship with a moral community. Thus, in the eyes of the state, the citizen, *like the madman* and *like the political dissident*, is in a perverse relationship to the normal order. The citizen and the radical have every reason to identify with the psychotic—on a basic level the state relates to them all in the same terms [that is, as things, objects, matter to be worked on and discarded]" (180).

What, of course, distinguishes the citizen and the political dissident from the madman is the command of the agency of language. Political outcasts are connected not only to the consensual world but to linguistic conventions that govern that world; therefore, they can manipulate power and position themselves with greater efficacy than can those for whom an internal *symbolic* dislocation has radically subverted conventions regarding the communicative transmission of signs. To understand the Other, to understand one's self in relation to the Other, is a basic requirement for staking out a position. The psychotic, the schizophrenic, is capable of only one kind of positioning: radical negation. But the act of negation itself has terribly destructive consequences. In its disorganization it leads to self-destruction. Language becomes an end not to political transformation or self-transformation but to an even greater confusion as to the boundaries between inside and outside.

Of course, the state objectifies both kinds of "dissidents"; but I think that the similarity ends there. At least political radicals or artistic outcasts know where they stand, what they want; the psychological refugee has no such command over competing realities that often shred the ego (witness the fate of host personas in multiple personalities).

Postmodernists on Capitalism and the Schizophrenic Self

The issue of volition or intention is as compelling as is language in the consideration of psychosis or madness. Deleuze and Guattari attribute a kind of political intentionality to the schizophrenic; it is as if, in their view, the schizophrenic acts out an internalized political or ideological program: "The schizophrenic deliberately seeks out the very limit of capitalism; he is its inherent tendency brought to fulfillment, its surplus product, its proletariat, and its exterminating angel. He scrambles all the codes and is the transmitter of the decoded flows of desire" (1977: 35). This may be something of what the schizophrenic is; the schizophrenic certainly "scrambles all the codes," what society designates as signs, rules, and context. But the scrambling is certainly not intentional. It is not a deliberative act, consciously undertaken as an assault on capitalism or capitalist ideology. Delusion and its logics define what the world is for the schizophrenic.

Nor is it at all clear that such selves transmit the "flows of desire." More likely, the schizophrenic self is a symbolic representation of the power of both internal and external forces to destroy desire and "flow." Delusion keeps the self riveted to an internal drama that defines how the self experiences what is occurring in the external or social world. Flow implies a movement outward, a connection, a dialectic; delusion is not dialectical; it enforces a rigidly contained reading of reality. If the schizophrenic's actions or language are political or ideological, they are so only because they are named as such by others. It is wildly misleading to suggest that the schizophrenic self has any conscious awareness that its delusional interpretations of "reality" possess any political significance. Delusion hardly renders the self socially functional or adept.

What distinguishes the schizophrenic is the profound *lack* of connection, the radical withdrawal from all forms of social exchange, the denial of consensual reality, the intense fear of intersubjectivity, and the hermetically sealed quality of delusion. Further, desire in delusion, rather than flowing outward to embodied others, takes on the grotesque form of omnipotent domination or chaotic victimization; desire is confined solely to the plane of delusion. It is not represented as a dialectical process. Rather, desire in the images of delusion appears to be symbolized statically. It is more like a concrete presence (blowing up the world—omnipotence; being blown up by the world—victimization) than like an uninterrupted flow.

Certainly the schizophrenic exists at the "limits of capitalism," in the sense that the schizophrenic mind is totally dysfunctional for the technological and rational tasks of capitalist organization. It is extraordinarily difficult for the schizophrenic to survive in sophisticated technological environments. In this respect, Deleuze and Guattari look at part of the truth: "Schizophrenia is a product of the capitalist machine, as manic depression and paranoia are the product of the despotic machine and hysteria the product of the territorial machine" (33). But these are catchy phrases or labels; they fail to describe what schizophrenia is, where manic depression comes from, what the sexualized roots of hysteria might be.

The person who is schizophrenic may be the product of terribly disturbed relations in the family, abnormal release or inhibition of chemicals in the brain, experiences generated during the first six months of life, genetic deficiencies, a "virus" contracted in utero. Although capitalism may enter into the etiological formulation, other factors exist which "explain" with equal plausibility and with, in some instances, more compelling evidence. It makes little sense to isolate capitalism or biology or family or fantasy as single-cause explanations if what each of these factors produce is a human being who suffers an extraordinary alienation from the symbolic world and leaps into the hermeticism of what Lacan calls the Imaginary and Kristeva calls "multiple sublations of the unnameable, the un-presentable, the void" (1986b: 300). Both multiple personalities and schizophrenics suffer from an extreme isolation: in the former, the compartmentalized quality of identity among the different alters, and in the latter, the total alienation of the fragmented self from any consensual relation with others outside the delusional frame.

Classical Concepts of Asylum

Where is consciousness to go to find refuge from what Turkle describes as the "perverse relationship to the normal order"? It is not an easy answer for the schizophrenic, wandering in a delusional placelessness, or for multiple personalities living in vast time warps and confusing absences or blackouts. No one place is recognizable as "safe," because the self functions according to logics that are either hidden and delusional (schizophrenia) or for the most part compartmentalized and separate (multiple personality).

How, then, might one proceed in at least making a dent in the Foucaultian, postmodernist position that sees institutions as part of an imprisoning set of epistemes, the "scientifico-disciplinary mechanisms" producing through "observation" and "surveillance" a "new technology of power and a new political anatomy of the body" (Foucault 1977: 193)? Might the notion of asylum, as a theory of refuge, as a place of safety for the persecuted or tormented self, possess a benefit for the psychically dislocated self—a benefit that transcends its ideological or philosophical interpretation?

Historically, cities of refuge, temples, and sacred places all possessed a ritualized function in ancient and primitive societies, offering safety to individuals thought to have committed an offense against nature, religion, or established political or tribal interests. Neither the state nor the law, however, felt any responsibility toward individuals perceived to be "mentally ill" (Rosen 1968: 121ff); asylum existed for political claimants suffering from persecution when powerful elements in the collective defined individuals or classes of individuals as unwanted or undesirable. The sole intention of the political concept of asylum lay in protecting the outcast and banished from retribution and vengeance; sanctuary defended the outlaw, the hunted, from political agents within the culture. Its purpose was "to mitigate the harshness of existing law. It acted as a corrective against the prevailing custom of considering the stranger a derelict and the slave completely open to mistreatment by his master" (Recht 1936: 5).

In its political incarnation asylum brought refuge from the unjust master, from political persecution, from religious strife, from the terror of living as a pariah and scapegoat. Asylum in its legal sense exercised a "particularly beneficial influence in view of the constant interstatal conflicts and intestine party strife, together with the universal practice of forced or voluntary banishment" (Phillipson 1911: 349). In its modern sense, according to legal opinion, asylum is a "right granted to a foreigner who cannot continue living in his own country because he is deprived of liberty, life or property by the political system prevailing there" (Sinha 1971: 176). Further, political asylum involves the "universal recognition, spontaneously and unconsciously arrived at, of the necessity to alleviate the rigour of the law, and of the obligation to extend mercy, under certain conditions, to those in distress, and more particularly to suppliant fugitives"[1] (Phillipson 1911: 347).

Why not extend these concepts to the protection of persons for whom the physical and linguistic connection with the world and experience finds itself distorted, cut off, and fragmented? Is not the psychological refugee a subject who experiences the world as torment? Might these juristic concepts, coming from a political past and tradition, be adapted to society's perception of the psychically displaced? The person beset by radical forms of psychological and emotional disconnection might legitimately make a claim for asylum as a form of sanctuary, as protection from the uncertainty of the normalizing society, from the felt experience of terror, even though the source of that terror lies in a private hidden knowledge, language,

---

[1] The political refugee leaves "nationality" because of "events occurring between that state and its citizens" (Sinha 1971: 278). A 1987 Supreme Court decision widened the latitude for the granting of asylum, claiming that "those seeking political asylum must prove only a 'well founded fear' of political persecution rather than a 'clear probability' of persecution should they be forced to return to their home countries" (*Washington Post*, March 17, 1987). If that ruling were to be extended to the psychically displaced, it would further enhance their argument for asylum from what the "normalizing" society brings as threat and fear.

or biology (the schizophrenic) or in split-off, screened memories presented to consciousness only through the alters or partial alters of multiple personalities.

Whatever the etiology of mental illness, society may have a moral obligation to grant asylum from suffering, a space of renewal, freedom, and tolerance, for the person who psychically runs from or denies the consensual world. Such a model of asylum might pattern itself on the ancient cities of refuge: places within the existing social system which would be considered safe havens—but in this instance a haven for persons "persecuted" by internal demons, memories from a tortured past or delusions haunting consciousness as persecutors.

The Psychological Refugee

In its classical form, political asylum served as a bulwark between the persecuted self and the social and cultural order; it stood against political definition of appropriate and inappropriate action. It offered refuge to religious and political factions. In its ideal formulation, it represented no special social interest or group; the effectiveness and respect for asylum depended on historic circumstances, on the good will of the established ruler, and on the prevailing status of political alignments. It posed a contradiction between what the fugitive self required and what society demanded; it enforced a distinction between the power of the reigning consensus and the needs of the individual seeking refuge.

In the context of this classical theory, the psychically displaced self becomes a psychological refugee from various social, political, and psychological constellations: the use and expression of language; instrumental rationality as power and domination; moral attitudes supporting theories of appropriateness; the requirements of political economy, particularly technological ones; the antipathy of the surrounding culture to dislocations in behavior and language; and in the case of women with multiple personality, the brutal demands of a phallocentric environment exceeding all forms of customary law.

The schizophrenic self, for example, is striking precisely because its psychological and biochemical disposition place it so at odds with a rational consensus that is hardly sympathetic: disheveled appearance, odd and bizarre language, the rejection of customary forms of thought, behavior that appears purposeless and occasionally anarchic, paralysis in negotiating the economic environment, the failure to be or do in terms the society acknowledges or rewards. The multiple personality exists in a universe where nothing can be assumed or taken for granted, where self possesses no fixed anchors, where even knowledge of self is prohibited because of the unique quality of alter personalities.

The consciousness of the schizophrenic is a lost consciousness; it occupies strange territories. It is hooked up to machines; it journeys to outer space; it experiences itself as connected to cosmic forces; it is an animal roaming the woods; it communicates with bees and flies. It finds bombs in transistor radios; it sees poison coming through the water; it hallucinates dead body parts strewn across the sky; it sees agents forming massive conspiracies whose sole purpose is to torture, murder, and dismember. In the truest sense, the schizophrenic lacks place. Homeless, alienated consciousness has been cast out of the social world, left adrift, without mooring or constancy. It is difficult to find or imagine a more psychically displaced human being than the schizophrenic. Jenny felt "three thousand years old," ancient, like a "mummy without flesh, just rotten stuff over my bones." She "coughed up worms" that ate away her eyes; she felt poisoned by "human" food and convinced herself that shampoo eroded her brain, that gases drifted out of the hospital air vents. Chuck saw himself as a "man beast, a turtle"; he believed his "teeth" stuck into his brain and his "feet" turned into "thousand-year-old nails."

It is quite commonplace to hear schizophrenics, and periodically those alter personalities "present" during traumatic periods of abuse, speak of themselves as things or objects to be used and depleted or broken up into bits and pieces. When Jenny conceives of herself as an animal carcass to be distributed to other patients, or Andrew feels "numbers" with gigantic jaws, swoop down from the heavens and threaten to eat him, or when "Leda" demands that Kimberly take her back to the cult for sacrifice, such beliefs or wishes remove the self from human association.

Culture Heroes or Mentally Ill?

Against the backdrop of such kinds of identifications, what sense
does it make to proclaim the schizophrenic, as Deleuze and Guattari
suggest, some kind of culture hero? Where is the heroic quality in
this utterance? It is more like pathos, a tragedy that carries with it
hopelessness and despair, without redemption. Beckett's characters
in *Endgame* living in barrels might be a literary equivalent. Deleuze
and Guattari write that "the schizophrenic process—in terms of
which the schizo is merely the interruption, or the continuation in
the void—is the potential for revolution" (341). But what kind of
revolution? How can persons who hallucinate, who live in fear, who
refuse to speak, who are desperately afraid of other persons, who
lack a sense of a historical self, be in any way considered "revolutionary"—a revolutionary for what! Deleuze and Guattari distort a
process that in its reality portrays loss, despair, impotence, and futility. The actual, physical face of madness is never shown in *Anti-
Oedipus*.

Deleuze and Guattari, in their analysis of "schizoanalysis," ignore the power of the psychological disconnection, internally held
forms of alienation, that deprive the self of its sense of efficacy and
worth. Eigen, for example, describes the effects of disconnection as
"ordering and disordering processes" which "are interwoven. Rigidity and chaos alternate, and boundaries are distorted or dissolve"
(1986: 2). The danger to identity here seems obvious: a boundary-
less self is a self without identity. For the political outcast, terror
comes from external agents; for the psychically disconnected, terror
radically disrupts internal forms of identification and knowledge. In
both instances, the effects are similar: a circumscribed existence in a
universe defined by terror.

This sense of existing without boundaries takes on frightening
proportions in the "multiplicity" of schizophrenia. For example,
Hilde, a thirty-two-year-old woman who has been hospitalized for
years, asks me, "How do I become a person? Maybe I should change
my eyes or move them differently or get new arms and toes? Do you
know where I can buy them? . . . Why don't you let me live inside
your skin; I can make myself real small and crawl right on in." These
are not utterances pointing toward a new symbolic integration, a

liberation, salvation or redemption. Hilde wanders in a placeless internal world whose only logics appear in the tragic images of delusion; she is as much without context or place as a political refugee.

The inner world of the mad self is a prison camp of a very special kind, and the plea "Who am I?" as compelling a demand for acknowledgment of place as a stateless person's despair over national identity. Both the stateless and the psychically displaced ask, "Where do I belong?" Each struggles on private and public planes with issues of boundary, constancy, identity, and fragmentation. Each confronts the reality of tyranny and constraint as commentary on what it means to experience refugeehood. The mad self faces a "normal" world that regards internal forms of derangement as contamination, infestation, and poison.

Girard's analysis of scapegoating may provide a useful perspective here. In myth, he argues, the victim may become the restorer, the healer of a terrible disaster that befalls the community; he redeems himself through action lauded as exemplary, noble, and selfless. But such restorations happen only in myth, which disguises or denies the truth of historical fact: "In myths, and only in myths, this same victim restores the order, symbolizes, and even incarnates it. . . . The greatest of all delinquencies is transformed into a pillar of society" (42). Is this transformation something of what Deleuze and Guattari are attempting with the schizophrenic: to see the victim as a hero, to mythologize what in reality is a process of extreme alienation and psychological pain?

Where, however, is the mythic quality in what society stigmatizes as disgusting, untouchable, and frightening? Persons who speak with animals, who try to burn themselves so that they will reach "God" or the spaceships, who try to slit their throats or who find themselves filled with compulsions to cut their flesh with razor blades or the tabs of soda cans, and who find pleasure in such acts, live and exist as psychological outcasts. It is difficult to find a poetry or a heroic quality in such actions; they are simply not transcendent or laudatory.

As I noted, Foucault, along with Deleuze and Guattari, believes that moral judgments derive from social practices whose objective lies in coercing speech and confining behavior; and Thomas Szasz also writes, "The assertion that a person is mentally ill involves rendering a moral judgment about him" (1970: 26). Yet are not certain states of "being" ill in some profound sense of that word? And why should the discovery or location of "illness" necessarily mean "moral judgment"? Sickness is in fact a real human condition.

If Ned tries to commit suicide because he feels his body is a hindrance to his final encounter with God, if a spirit in his head tells him his flesh is bad and must be ripped out, or if Nora screams that because the cult is out to sacrifice her she must die to prevent mutilation of her body or the capture of her daughter, is the attribution of "illness" to such utterance a moral judgment? Or if Jenny spends half a day eating grass on the hospital grounds because she believes herself to be a cow and has to "feed" her "unborn calves" or if Molly spends evenings burning her arms, unaware in the morning how such burns got there, is interpreting these states of mind as an "illness" a question of moral judgment? Julia writes in her diary, "I am sick, so very sick, someone help me please, help!" Is she lying to herself; is she really not sick? Is carving in her leg with a razor blade the words "Dear Mom, I love you all" a minor problem in adaptation, the consequence of capitalist territories and prevailing social practices?

Chuck experiences a real and discernible detachment from the human species; is this an illness? Is it productive, useful, normal, "healthy," for a person to feel as if he is three billion years old, that he lives in "suspended animation," that he has been put on "ice cubes" for centuries, that a computer located in Honduras controls his actions and thoughts? How does one understand Liz, who remained mute for an entire year and when she finally began to speak described her silence as a screen for a hallucinatory inner world keeping her continually preoccupied—for example, seeing Christmas tree bulbs as shrunken human heads, or dodging flying knives that chased her around the hall?

The attribution of illness may imply more than a question of judgment. If to be ill is to face the world with a terrorized consciousness, to live according to logics that have nothing to do with consensual understandings, then psychological or mental illness may be a very real and palpable phenomenon.

The psychically displaced person, never voluntarily chooses to go crazy; it is absurd to think that anyone would willingly choose to be schizophrenic, to live under a constant regime of psychological torture. This experience is much different from the hallucinogenic or mystical experience of reaching a "higher" or more "transcendent" reality, of taking the self out of time—for a moment. There is nothing mystical about the disintegrative presence of schizophrenia; nor does one simply step out of being schizophrenic. What is clear, however, is that society imputes to such persons an otherness that excludes and demonstrates an insensitivity to the causes provoking these unsettling representations of human action and desire.

Asylum in the Context of Scapegoating

Consider that for the psychological refugee the idea of the "state" or of "nationality" functions as an accumulation of beliefs, feelings, and expectations that inhere in the internalized projections of delusion, or, in the case of the multiple personality, in the static presence of each alter's identity. It is the "state" experienced not as a definable national or historical entity (a "nation" among other "nations") but as the "state" or "regime" that works on consciousness, as it exists within the mind. The operation of that "state" or, better, "authority" ("authorities" in the case of the multiple personality) may appear as a compendium of voices, hallucinations, or traits controlling behavior, thought, and action—internal perceptions bringing persistent and unyielding pain. It is as if multiplicity in the form of delusion or alter personalities had evolved into an internalized law: what functions as law, power, authority, and justice appears in the images and logics of delusional projections or, with the multiple personality, in the unrelated and disconnected personality traits of alters, particularly persecutory alters. In a political sense, what matters for these persons is the exclusionary force of multiplicity, supported by the collective, removing the self from connection and participation in a historically given *civitas*. That exclusionary process can be as vicious and unyielding as the forced banishment of the political exile or the effects of the brain's chemical, neurophysiological interactions. Asylum, then, for the mentally ill would involve efforts to diminish the hold of delusion or multiplicity, to break up the rigidity of terror which grips the self caught in nonhistorically defined frames of reference or epistemologies, and to create the therapeutic conditions for the emergence of a self capable of withstanding life in a socially constituted environment.

Asylum could also educate the community about the despair and suffering inherent in psychological alienation; it could help to demystify the collective's fear. The consensual world finds little place for those who identify with objects, things, or animals, identities of a bizarre or haunting otherness. Such forms of identification, especially acute in schizophrenics, bring derision, fear, or, at the worst, banishment from existing social contexts. Banishment of the mentally ill from the rational consensus has a long history. An example from the perspective of a classical Roman describes identification with the nonhuman or nonconsensual world: "One victim of madness fancied himself a sparrow, another a cock, another an earthen vessel, another a brick, another a god, another an orator, another a tragic actor, another a comic actor, another a stalk of grain and asserted that he occupied the center of the universe, and another cried like a baby and begged to be carried in the arms." Or, in the words of the observer "Arateus": "[Harmless madmen . . . are] given to extraordinary phantasies; for one is afraid of the fall of the oil cruets . . . and another will not drink, as fancying himself a brick, and fearing lest he should be dissolved by the liquid" (both quoted in Rosen 1968: 97).

Is it inevitable that society needs its mad people, without regard as to what causes or precipitates "madness"? Are these representations of the scapegoat, the other, the negative in the culture, actually "languages" that describe what the collective fears most in itself? If this is true, then in granting asylum to those who for whatever psychological reason possess the "demonic" (whether in delusion or, in the case of the multiple personality, persecuting, sadistic alters), the culture acknowledges a fragile yet very real dimension of its own existence, the vulnerability of the collective, its own complicity in both madness and, through its exclusionary process, victimization.

Girard's analysis adds an important dimension: the psychically displaced person's perception of self as animal is enforced by the crowd that may perceive or transform its victims into animals, other-than-human, perhaps one of the psychological dynamics behind cult practices of human sacrifice. "The gradual disappearance of the borderline between animal and man in those who are marked as victims is an important concept" (48). Witches, for example, who managed a stableful of animals were often perceived as animals themselves; is it any different with the delusional self, or the human in cult sacrifice whose status is similar to that of chickens and goats?

Chuck identifies with a dog, a cheetah, a bird. Might these identifications have something to do with social perceptions that surround the self's existential field, messages the society sends to the estranged self, the mirror relationship of doubles? If society has seen animality and unreason in such persons, it is understandable that the self might then internalize such perceptions as its own. Girard calls this process "mimesis": "If the alleged witch possesses a pet, a cat, a dog, or a bird, she is immediately thought to resemble that animal, and the animal itself seems almost an incarnation, a temporary embodiment or a useful disguise to ensure the success of certain enterprises" (48).

Chuck frequently likes to walk alone on the hospital grounds, because in that environment he talks to the dogs. Yet not only does his internal self speak the language and assume the identity of animals; society also names Chuck as other-than-human, as animal-like, although Chuck-the-animal is not put on public display, as he might have been in the eighteenth century. Chuck and the social world mirror each other; for Chuck to understand himself as animal depends in large measure on how the social world perceives him. It is a reciprocal relationship of doubles. To seek asylum, then, involves taking refuge not only from the internal terrors of one's own madness (which possess their own special reality) but from the shared quality, the mimetic presence of that madness in the collective itself.

Asylum: Prison or Refuge?

What the consensual world offers as "treatment" (institutions, therapists, medications—all agents of the social interest), the psychically displaced self may understand as poison or threat.

For the multiple personality, treatment becomes threatening to those alters who wish to destroy the host or return to the cult or who possess a sadistic quality bent on inflicting pain. For some schizophrenics, the holding environment of the hospital may block suicidal wishes. For example, internal psychological percepts may lead the self to want to "leave" the body and "join" the spaceships, as Eddy did, and the route for this escape may be a wish to ignite his body in flames because smoke travels more quickly than flesh and "smoke goes up." Therefore, as Eddy put it, to "go up" in smoke means literally to join the spaceships; the body dissolved into smoke will drift upward. To prevent Eddy from burning himself, the society, in the form of psychiatrist or institution, may prescribe medications, restraints, twenty-four-hour nursing, and so on. Even though Eddy may experience these actions as restraints, society makes the choice to save Eddy's life rather than to permit his enactment of the delusional drama. Similarly with Nora: when she is strapped into the Geri chair, it is almost impossible for her to hurt herself during traumatic flashbacks. Also, contained within the hospital, she finds protection from the cult, or what she understands to be the cult's wishes toward her.

It may be misleading to condemn, without qualification, all institutions that care for what I have been calling psychological disconnection. Institutions may only confine, or they may offer both confinement and asylum. Or specific persons or units within an institutional environment may function, because of personality, belief, and commitment, as asylum in an otherwise "normalizing" institution. It would be unfair, particularly for persons who require some form of containment, who are suicidal or self-destructive, or who feel murderous toward others, to condemn institutions as a matter of ideological fiat. Would Deleuze and Guattari have increasing bands of homeless people, intolerable physical suffering, higher rates of suicide—the obvious consequences of physical and emotional neglect? Yet it would also be wrong to accept institutional readings of reality exclusively; institutions can in fact be oppressive. In this sense the idea or ideal of asylum might be a clarifying dynamic in those institutions that society designates for the purpose of holding or containing "madness." We should question institutions constantly to ask whether, in fact, treatment acknowledges the language of the illness, allows its expression, and offers to encounter illness without conceiving of it as an aberrant pathogenic presence to be managed, repressed, sealed over, and treated. Although institutions or parts of them may or may not function in the classical sense of providing refuge and safety, the theoretical point remains valid: confinement (which may be a misuse of social power) and asylum (which may be a true refuge from torment) do not necessarily mean the same thing.

The psychically displaced self may face a terrible paradox: it may see external agents as persecutory, but it also may be haunted by internal percepts of delusion, taunting voices, or angry, sadistic alters. The normalizing, external world holds threat and the internal world tyrannizes and terrorizes. Delusion, or multiplicity as forms of internal power, has displaced social and consensual reality, but because of its terrorizing presence, it obviously fails to bring a true asylum. To live with the spaceships, to manage imaginary wars, to be wandering around fantasized deserts, to harbor unknown but very real personalities, hardly brings refuge. Is it any wonder, given this "no exit" desperate condition, that a voice or personality may suggest forms of self-immolation: burning, hanging, cutting, or shooting?

The question of the psychological refugee "Where do I belong?" is a compelling one about both place and identity. If the self responds by defining "belonging" as being a star in the galaxy, or a three-thousand-year-old petrified mummy, or the captain of a fleet of outer-space vessels, or the ruler of the universe, or a messenger from Satan, or the host personality presiding over a house of alters, what is being said is a statement about place. In forsaking the social life world because of its pain, consciousness, in locating meaning or being within these kinds of constructions, leaves social or consensual forms of knowledge behind. Yet the practical consequences of this exit is a falling into refugeehood, a perverse relationship to the normal order and its consensual assumptions.

It is a tragic form of disintegration, this placelessness, so obvious in the delusional nothingness of schizophrenia and the fear of such alters as Elizabeth, who know that ultimately they will be banished to the "fog." "Where do I belong? In what world am I a citizen?" describes something of the dilemma. "Do I belong in trees, in spaceships, in cities underneath the hospital, in migrations through China, at the end of the torturer's knife? Am I a body without a brain, God's emissary on earth, a rock star, a promoter staging ten thousand concerts a day? Where do I belong? Which persona is mine: am I Leda, Elizabeth, Tink, Jenny Precious, Kimberly?" To be, as Molly puts it, "lost to time," or, in Elizabeth's terms, "a presence from the fog," is to be an outcast to history. It is to be without place, without historical being. It is to live outside the psychological boundaries of the *civitas* and to see civil society as full of pain, harboring agents who seek the self's annihilation. And the last place the psychological refugee wants to be, in the midst of a delusional panic or terrifying flashback, is in the malevolent "normal" world with real human beings and their insistent, often brutal, demands for intimacy.

The paradox is tragic, almost insoluble: the self seeks to escape the consensual world, yet where else is it to live? In delusion? In a medicated stupor, locked away in a back ward? In a dingy room in a rundown section of the city? In an existential horror where the appearance of alters makes a mockery of the concept of freedom and self-knowledge?

If society accepts the human costs of placelessness, and its psychological variations, then asylum need not be a concern. If those costs manifest themselves in human destruction, in suicide, in psychological starvation, in the dislocations of family, then the social world or "normalizing" society has decided that it is cheaper or more cost-effective to live with those costs. Not only the community but the philosophers of postmodernism seem to have consigned such individuals to the "dustbin" of history.

CONCLUSION:

THE PARADOXICAL
PLIGHT OF FRAGMENTED
AND MULTIPLE SELVES

To be delusional or to suffer from multiple personality, yet also to function in the consensual world, is to live in a dilemma. It is to suffer at the hands of power; it is to contain within oneself a radical confusion as to the nature of being and identity; and it is to be misunderstood by society. The multiple personality does function; a consciousness lives in the world, but which one depends on which persona or identity is present to consensual reality. Multiple personality disorder is not a psychotic condition, yet the several states of mind create radical forms of disintegration and emotional chaos which work themselves out both on the body and in self-representations living in the midst of society. In both instances—multiple personality and psychosis (in which consciousness lives within a framework defined by internal delusional projections totally dissociated from externality)—the human being suffers from an alienation so intense that life itself becomes a continuing journey into pain.

The postmodern critics of psychoanalysis in their celebration of multiplicity rarely acknowledge this suffering. It is as if they are saying that the pain simply does not matter, that what is important is the political meaning these human beings offer for ideological argument and for attacks against institutionalism, psychiatric categorization, and the normalizing society. They do not acknowledge that such persons simply do not have the capacity to become artists or eloquent poets; there is little eloquence in the utterances of the mad or in the torments of women suffering horrifying flashbacks. These persons could not live with the demands of a revolutionary *praxis* attached to their suffering. The critics dangerously lose sight of the person: is not a fitting object of social theory the status of the self, its physical and psychological body? Is it not equally as important to understand and interpret the world from the point of view of the victims themselves? Are people not as important as texts? Where are the *victims'* voices in the nihilistic critiques of such theorists as Deleuze and Guattari and, more broadly, postmodernists such as Baudrillard and Lyotard? Are texts and letters the only phenomena that count? The pain and indeterminacy of human suffering for these critics, the literal horrors of victimhood and survivorhood, remain in the background, secondary considerations in the postmodernist idealization of multiplicity.

The recognition of the importance of a coherent historical self and of a theory of asylum would propose the preparation of the tormented self for life in an existing, historically defined consensual world, with all its imperfections. No retreat can be permanent; there is no ultimate escape from the normalizing society, except perhaps death, which both schizophrenics and multiple personalities often find intriguing and seductive, as did the hostile alters in Nora and Kimberly. There are no utopias for the psychically displaced, nor does any evidence support the conclusion that dissociated selves would in fact desire some kind of utopia. To become aware of what one carries inside—that is, to initiate the process of deconstructing delusion in schizophrenia, an almost impossible therapeutic task even with the use of appropriate medication, or to resolve the separable and fused personas of a multiple personality—is to gain a knowledge of the world as a place of imperfection, struggle, and hope.

That is certainly a form of knowledge quite different from Deleuze and Guattari's idealized and sanitized version of psychological liberation. One of the most remarkable absences in their book is any reflection on the pain carried not only in the language of the schizophrenic but in the body itself. Is not the recognition of physical pain, produced by psychological forms of torture, vital to any realistic theory of the self?

Schizophrenics and multiple personalities who manage to function in the consensual world describe aspiration in the language of the normalizing society. They express a wish to be left alone and not be reminded of what they have experienced. Their objectives point directly to a "normal" life; they see themselves not as symbols for more generalized political arguments over insight and specialness. They talk about jobs, skill development, and education. If, in fact, the psychically displaced hate their specialness and crave normality, then such hopes run up against the postmodern critics' ideological call for the decentered self and the use of the schizophrenic, in the case of Deleuze and Guattari, as a symbol of protest against capitalist society and its forms of knowledge/power.

My look at asylum—as a refuge and as a place for integrating the self—from the perspective of the self desperately needing it, is an effort to come to terms with terrors, demons, or personalities occupying consciousness. It is a call for safety, peace, retreat, a space to climb out of despair—nothing more. It is not a call for an extraordinary revolution in consciousness; to be in "asylum" is not to be in a group, institution, or place completely cut off from society; it is not a denial of the surrounding world. It is, however, an argument that demands a certain empathy from prevailing social power and its sites in the community.

Asylum is a plea to be allowed to rediscover what is human and constant inside the self, to learn how to trust other human beings, and to be able to feel and express some degree of tenderness and closeness without being overwhelmed by fears of fusion, annihilation, and dismemberment. These interpersonal modes of being, critical to the creation of a historically rooted identity, constitute and have constituted for the delusional self and the multiple personality enormous threat. Is it any wonder why these persons shy away from being considered "special"?

Yet I acknowledge that part of the appeal of such theorists as Deleuze and Guattari, and Foucault is that their critique contains an important part of the truth in casting the schizophrenic as the victim of twisted, power-hungry institutions and discourses. Also valuable is Girard's argument that "madness" is a state of mind or being which represents a split-off or denied aspect of the collective "truth" and that the language of madness reveals what the collective often denies in itself.

To recognize that the "mad" and the "sane" constitute part of each other, that the collective and its demons derive from a shared human nature, assigns to madness a quality that makes it more than a politically defined label or an artificial construct. It is real, a terrifying place, one that is palpable and "there," a vivid presence in the collective dynamics of human experience. The madness of the group, the group cult, the group state, the group nation, is as terrifying as the solitary self screaming at the moon, fighting invisible demons, or carving up an imaginary body.

Louis, a thirty-two-year-old schizophrenic, lives in a world of murderous rage, of extreme loneliness, and with a profound distrust of all human beings. He sees himself as a "wild beast"; he wants to shoot me so that he might live. He expresses a fantasy of taking my "human blood" into his "animal veins," puncturing holes in my neck with his "canine teeth." Everything, all life, assaults Louis. Even silence becomes intolerable because the "stillness of things feels like a sledgehammer rattling the inside of my brain." Louis says to me, "You're psychotic, crazy, a killer, you want to smash the hell out of me . . . blow my brains out, eat them for your dinner. . . . I hate your guts. . . . If I had a knife I'd slit you from head to toe and then cut you up into little pieces and feed you to the dogs."

Yet, what part of Louis is society? To what extent is his rage an example of what exists in the collective, what is expressed in political form, political "rage," what Vamik Volkan (1988) speaks about as the need to have enemies? To what extent is what Louis expresses in language embedded psychically in institutions, in their form and intent? To what extent is what is written on Nora's body a projection of deranged collective forms of modernism taking shape in hidden places in which patriarchal power writes its brutality without restraint?

In this sense Girard's notion of the "mirror of doubles" amplifies the psychological and historical context of what madness signifies for the larger group or culture. If madness of the self or the deranged madness of unrestrained power is not an aberrant condition but a potential or tendency in the collective, an aspect of human nature shattering socialized limits and boundaries, then Louis and Nora become more than pathogenic presences. They reveal the psychological underside of power, its embeddedness in the family, its complicity in the destruction and death of the self, its pathogenesis in delusion, its attachment to the collective will, and its alliance with patriarchal oppression. But to see the schizophrenic or the multiple personality as culture heroes, as carriers of a new "postmodern" synthesis, as symbols of a nihilist awakening, is to mystify and distort what they and the circumstances of their respective tragedies speak.

REFERENCES

Alford, C. F. 1989. *Melanie Klein and Critical Social Theory: An Account of Politics, Art, and Reason Based on Her Psychoanalytic Theory*. New Haven: Yale University Press.

——. 1991. *The Self in Social Theory: A Psychoanalytic Account of Its Construction in Plato, Hobbes, Locke, Rawls, and Rousseau*. New Haven: Yale University Press.

——. 1992. *The Psychoanalytic Theory of Greek Tragedy: Humane Antihumanism*. New Haven: Yale University Press.

Augustine. 1963. *The Trinity*. Trans. S. McKennan. Washington, D.C.: Catholic University of America Press.

Baldwin, L. 1984. *Ourselves: Multiple Personalities, 1811–1981*. London: McFarland.

Barthes, R. 1975. *The Pleasure of the Text*. Trans. R. Miller. New York: Hill and Wang.

Bataille, G. 1985. *Visions of Excess: Selected Writings, 1929–1939*. Ed. Allan Stoekl. Minneapolis: University of Minnesota Press.

Baudrillard, J. 1983. *In the Shadow of the Silent Majorities*. New York: Semiotext, Columbia University Press.

——. 1984a. "Game with Vestiges." *On the Beach* 5 (Winter): 19–25.

——. 1984b. "On Nihilism." *On the Beach* 6 (Spring): 38–39.

——. 1987. *Forget Foucault*. New York: Semiotext, Columbia University Press.

——. 1988. *Selected Writings*. Ed. M. Poster. Stanford, Calif.: Stanford University Press.

Beahrs, J. O. 1982. "Unity and Multiplicity: Multilevel Consciousness of Self." In Beahrs, ed., *Hypnosis, Psychiatric Disorder, and Mental Health*. New York: Brunner/Mazel, 1982.

Benhabib, S. 1990. "Epistemologies of Postmodernism: A Rejoinder to Jean-François Lyotard." In L. J. Nicholson, ed., *Feminism/Postmodernism*. New York: Routledge, 1990.

Benjamin, W. 1969. *Illuminations*. Ed. H. Arendt. New York: Schocken.

Bennett, T. 1982. "Text and History." In P. Widdowson, ed., *Rereading English*. New York: Methuen, 1982.

Bion, W. R. 1959. *Experience in Groups and Other Papers*. New York: Basic Books.

Bliss, E. L. 1986. *Multiple Personality, Allied Disorders, and Hypnosis*. New York: Oxford University Press.

Bliss, E. L. 1989. "Spontaneous Self Hypnosis in Multiple Personality Disorder." *Psychiatric Clinics of North America* 7:1.

Brennan, T., ed. 1989. *Between Feminism and Psychoanalysis*. New York: Routledge.

Cixous, H. 1974. "The Character of 'Character.'" Trans. K. Cohen. *New Literary History* 5: 383–402.

——. 1981. "Castration or Decapitation." Trans. A. Kuhn. *Signs* 7: 41–55.

——. 1985. *Angst*. Trans. J. Levy. New York: Riverrun Press.

——. 1986. *Inside*. Trans. C. Barko. New York: Schocken.

——. 1990. "Difficult Joys." In H. Wilcox, K. McWatters, A. Thompson, L. R. Williams, eds., *The Body and the Text: Hélène Cixous, Reading and Teaching*. New York: St. Martin's Press, 1990.

Cixous, H., and C. Clément. 1986. "The Newly Born Woman." Trans. B. Wing. In *Theory and History of Literature* 24. Minneapolis: University of Minnesota Press, 1986.

Conley, V. A. 1984. *Hélène Cixous, Writing the Feminine*. Lincoln: University of Nebraska Press.

Cooley, C. H. 1964. *Human Nature and the Social Order*. New York: Schocken.

Cooper, D. 1971. *Sanity, Madness, and the Family*. New York: Penguin.

Corlett, W. 1989. *Community without Unity: A Politics of Derridian Extravagance*. Durham, N.C.: Duke University Press.

Crabtree, A. 1985. *Multiple Man: Explorations in Possession and Multiple Personality*. New York: Praeger.

Deleuze, G. 1971. *Sacher-Masoch: An Interpretation*. Trans. J. McNeil. London: Faber and Faber.

Deleuze, G., and F. Guattari. 1977. *Anti-Oedipus: Capitalism and Schizophrenia*. Trans. R. Harley, M. Seem, and H. R. Lane. New York: Viking, 1972.

Derrida, J. 1978. *Writing and Difference*. Trans. A. Bass. Chicago: University of Chicago Press.

Di Stefano, C. 1990. "Dilemmas of Difference." In L. J. Nicholson, ed., *Feminism/Postmodernism*. New York: Routledge.

Eagleton, T. 1983. *Literary Theory: An Introduction*. Minneapolis: University of Minnesota Press.

Eigen, M. 1986. *The Psychotic Core*. Northvale, N.J.: Jason Aronson.

Evans, M. N. 1987. *Masks of Tradition: Women and the Politics of Writing in Twentieth Century France*. Ithaca: Cornell University Press.

Fairbairn, W. R. D. 1944. "Endopsychic Structure Considered in Terms of Object-Relationships." In Fairbairn, *Psychoanalytic Studies of the Personality*. Boston: Routledge and Kegan Paul, 1952.

Federman, R. 1975. "Surfiction—Four Propositions in Form of an Introduction."

In Federman, ed., *Surfiction: Fiction Now and Tomorrow*. Chicago: Swallow Press, 1975.

——. 1978. "Fiction Today, or the Pursuit of Non-Knowledge." *Humanities in Society* 1 (Spring): 115–32.

Feldstein, R., and J. Roof, eds. 1989. *Feminism and Psychoanalysis*. Ithaca: Cornell University Press.

Flax, J. 1987. "Postmodernism and Gender Relations in Feminist Theory." In M. R. Malson, J. F. O'Barr, S. Westphal-Wihl, and M. Wyler, eds., *Feminist Theory in Practice and Process*. Chicago: University of Chicago Press, 1989.

——. 1990. *Thinking Fragments: Psychoanalysis, Feminism, and Post-Modernism in the Contemporary West*. Berkeley: University of California Press.

Foucault, M. 1965. *Madness and Civilization*. Trans. R. Howard. New York: Random House.

——. 1976. *Mental Illness and Psychology*. Trans. A. Sheridan. New York: Harper and Row.

——. 1977. *Discipline and Punishment: The Birth of the Prison*. Trans. A. Sheridan. New York: Vintage.

——. 1978. *The History of Sexuality*, vol. 1: *An Introduction*. Trans R. Hinley. New York: Pantheon.

Fraser, N. 1989. *Unruly Practices: Power, Discourse, and Gender in Contemporary Social Theory*. Minneapolis: University of Minnesota Press.

Fraser, N., and L. J. Nicholson. 1990. "Social Criticism without Philosophy." In L. J. Nicholson, ed., *Feminism/Postmodernism*. New York: Routledge, 1990.

Frosh, S. 1987. *The Politics of Psychoanalysis: An Introduction to Freudian and Post-Freudian Theory*. New Haven: Yale University Press.

Gaggi, S. 1989. *Modern/Postmodern: A Study in Twentieth-Century Arts and Ideas*. Philadelphia: University of Pennsylvania Press.

Gallop, J. 1982a. *The Daughter's Seduction: Feminism and Psychoanalysis*. Ithaca: Cornell University Press.

——. 1982b. *Reading Lacan*. Ithaca: Cornell University Press.

Gilman, S. L. 1985. *Difference and Pathology: Stereotypes of Sexuality, Race, and Madness*. Ithaca: Cornell University Press.

Girard, R. 1986. *The Scapegoat*. Baltimore: Johns Hopkins University Press.

Glass, J. 1985. *Delusion: Internal Dimensions of Political Life*. Chicago: University of Chicago Press.

——. 1987. "Schizophrenia and Rationality: On the Function of the Unconscious Fantasy." In D. Levin, ed., *Modern Pathologies of the Self*. New York: New York University Press, 1987.

——. 1989. *Private Terror/Public Life: Psychosis and the Politics of Community*. Ithaca: Cornell University Press.

Goffman, E. 1961. *Asylums*. New York: Doubleday Anchor.

Grosz, E. 1990. *Jacques Lacan: A Feminist Introduction*. New York: Routledge.

Harding, S. 1986. *The Science Question in Feminism*. Ithaca: Cornell University Press.

Hawthorn, J. 1983. *Multiple Personality and the Disintegration of Literary Character*. New York: St. Martin's Press.

Herman, J. L. 1992. *Trauma and Recovery: The Aftermath of Violence—from Domestic Abuse to Political Terror.* New York: Basic Books.

Horevitz, R. P., and B. G. Braun. 1984. "Are Multiple Personalities Borderline?" *Psychiatric Clinics of North America* 7(1).

Hoy, D. C., ed. 1986. *Foucault: A Critical Reader.* New York: Basil Blackwell.

Humphrey, N., and D. C. Dennett. 1989. "Speaking for Ourselves: An Assessment of Multiple Personality Disorder." *Raritan* 9 (Summer): 68–98.

Huyssen, A. 1990. "Mapping the Postmodern." In L. J. Nicholson, ed., *Feminism/Postmodernism.* New York: Routledge.

Irigaray, L. 1985a. *This Sex Which Is Not One.* Trans. C. Porter with C. Burke. Ithaca: Cornell University Press.

Irigaray, L. 1985b. *Speculum of the Other Woman.* Trans. G. Gill. Ithaca: Cornell University Press.

Janet, P. 1907. *The Major Systems of Hysteria.* New York: Macmillan.

Jardine, A. A. 1985. *Gynesis: Configurations of Woman and Modernity.* Ithaca: Cornell University Press.

Kafka, F. 1904. *Correspondences.* Quoted in Cixous 1990.

Kariel, H. 1989. *The Desperate Politics of Postmodernism.* Amherst: University of Massachusetts Press.

Kellner, D. 1988. "Postmodernism as Social Theory: Some Challenges and Problems." *Theory, Culture, and Society* (London: SAGE), 5: 39–69.

Klein, M. 1946. "Notes on Some Schizoid Mechanisms." In J. Riviere, ed., *Development in Psychoanalysis.* London: Hogarth Press, 1952.

Kluft, R. P. 1984, March. "Treatment of Multiple Personality Disorder: A Study of 33 Cases." *Psychiatric Clinics of North America* 7(1).

Kohut, H. 1971. *The Analysis of the Self.* New York: International Universities Press.

——. 1977. *The Restoration of the Self.* New York: International Universities Press.

——. 1985. *Self Psychology and the Humanities.* New York: Norton.

Kristeva, J. 1974. "Revolution in Poetic Language." Trans. M. Waller. In T. Moi, ed., *The Kristeva Reader: Julia Kristeva.* New York: Columbia University Press, 1986.

——. 1980. "Word, Dialogue and Novel." In L. S. Roudiez, ed., *Desire in Language: A Semiotic Approach to Literature and Art.* Trans. T. Gora, A. Jardine, and L. S. Roudiez. New York: Columbia University Press.

——. 1981. "Women's Time." Trans. A. Jardine and H. Blake. In T. Moi, ed., *The Kristeva Reader: Julia Kristeva.* New York: Columbia University Press, 1986.

——. 1982. *Psychoanalysis and the Polis.* Trans. M. Waller. In T. Moi, ed., *The Kristeva Reader: Julia Kristeva.* New York: Columbia University Press, 1986.

——. 1986a. "The True/Real." Trans. S. Hand. In T. Moi, ed., *The Kristeva Reader: Julia Kristeva.* New York: Columbia University Press, 1986.

——. 1986b. "Freud and Love: Treatment and Its Discontents." Trans. L. S. Roudiez. In T. Moi, ed., *The Kristeva Reader: Julia Kristeva.* New York: Columbia University Press.

——. 1986c. "A New Type of Intellectual: The Dissident." Trans. S. Hand. In T. Moi, ed., *The Kristeva Reader: Julia Kristeva.* New York: Columbia University Press.

———. 1987. *In the Beginning Was Love; Psychoanalysis and Faith.* Trans. A. Goldhammer. New York: Columbia University Press.

———. 1989. *Language, the Unknown: An Initiation into Linguistics.* Trans. A. M. Menke. New York: Columbia University Press.

Kroker, A., and D. Cook. 1986. *The Postmodern Scene: Excremental Culture and Hyper-Aesthetics.* New York: St. Martin's Press.

Lacan, J. 1968. *The Language of the Self: The Function of Language in Psychoanalysis.* Trans. A. Wilden. New York: Dell.

———. 1977. "The Function and Field of Speech and Language in Psychoanalysis." In J. Lacan, *Ecrits: A Selection.* London: Tavistock.

———. 1982. *Feminine Sexuality: Jacques Lacan and the école freudienne.* Ed. J. Mitchell and J. Rose. New York: Norton.

Laing, R. D. 1978. *The Divided Self.* New York: Penguin.

———. 1980. *Sanity, Madness, and the Family.* New York: Penguin.

Lawson, H., and L. Appignanesi, eds. 1989. *Dismantling Truth: Reality in the Post-Modern World.* New York: St. Martin's Press.

Lyotard, J. F. 1988. *The Differend: Phrases in Dispute.* Trans. G. V. D. Abbule. Minneapolis: University of Minnesota Press.

———. 1989. "The Postmodern Condition: A Report on Knowledge." Trans. G. Bennington and B. Massumi. *Theory and History of Literature 10.* Minneapolis: University of Minnesota Press, 1989.

McCormick, R. M. 1991. *Politics of the Self: Feminism and the Postmodern in West German Literature and Film.* Princeton, N.J.: Princeton University Press.

Mahler, M., F. Pine, and A. Bergman. 1975. *The Psychological Birth of the Human Infant.* New York: Basic Books.

Masson, J. 1984. *Assault on Truth: Freud's Suppression of the Sanction Theory.* New York: Farrar, Straus, and Giroux.

Mead, G. H. 1934. *Mind, Self, and Society from the Standpoint of a Social Behaviorist.* Ed. C. W. Norris. Chicago: University of Chicago Press.

Miller, N. K. 1988. *Subject to Change: Reading Feminist Writing.* New York: Columbia University Press.

Miller, N. K., ed. 1986. *The Poetics of Gender.* New York: Columbia University Press.

Mitchell, J. 1984. *Women: The Longest Revolution.* New York: Pantheon.

Moi, T. 1986. "Introduction." In T. Moi, ed., *The Kristeva Reader: Julia Kristeva.* New York: Columbia University Press, 1986.

———. 1989. "Patriarchal Thought and the Drive for Knowledge." In T. Brennan, ed., *Between Psychoanalysis and Feminism.* New York: Routledge.

Morris, M. 1988. *The Pirate's Fiancé: Feminism, Reading, Postmodernism.* New York: Verso.

Nicholson, L. J., ed. 1990. *Feminism/Postmodernism.* New York: Routledge.

Nietzsche, F. 1968. *The Will to Power.* Trans. W. Kaufmann and R. J. Hollingale. New York: Vintage.

Pateman, C. 1988. *The Sexual Contract.* Stanford, Calif.: Stanford University Press.

Pavel, T. G. 1990. *The Feud of Language: A History of Structuralist Thought.* Oxford: Blackwell.

Pfeil, F. 1988. "Potholders and Subincisions." In E. Ann Kaplan, ed., *Postmodernism and Its Discontents*. New York: Verso, 1988.

Phillipson, C. 1911. *The International Law and Custom of Ancient Greece and Rome*. London: Macmillan.

Prince, M. 1906. *The Dissociation of a Personality: A Biographical Study in Abnormal Psychology*. London and New York: Longmans, Green.

Putnam, F. W. 1989. *Diagnosis and Treatment of Multiple Personality Disorder*. New York: Guilford Press.

Putnam, F., J. Guroff, E. Silverman, L. Barber, and R. Poso. 1986. "The Clinical Phenomenon of Multiple Personality Disorder in Recent Cases." *Journal of Clinical Psychiatry* 47: 285–93.

Ragland-Sullivan, E. 1986. *Jacques Lacan and the Philosophy of Psychoanalysis*. Chicago: University of Illinois Press.

Recht, C. 1936. *The Right of Asylum*. New York: The Social Economic Foundation Inc.

Rivera, M. 1989. "Linking the Psychological and the Social: Feminism, Post-Structuralism, and Multiple Personality." *Dissociation* 9 (March): 24–31.

Rorty, R. 1989. "Science as Solidarity." In H. Lawson, and L. Appignanesi, eds., *Dismantling Truth: Reality in the Post-Modern World*. New York: St. Martin's Press, 1989.

Rosen, G. 1968. *Madness in Society*. London: Routledge and Kegan Paul.

Ross, C., B. Norton, and K. Wozney. 1989. "Multiple Personality Disorder: An Analysis of 236 Cases." *Canadian Journal of Psychiatry* 34: 413–18.

Ryan, M. 1988. "Post Modern Politics." *Theory, Culture and Society* 5 (June): 2–3.

Sankovitch, T. A. 1988. *French Women Writers and the Book: Myths of Access and Desire*. Syracuse, N.Y.: Syracuse University Press.

Schaefer, R. 1968. *Aspects of Internalization*. New York: International Universities Press.

Schechner, R. 1982. *The End of Humanism: Writings on Performance*. New York: Performing Arts Journal Publications.

Searles, H. 1960. *The Non-Human Environment*. New York: International Universities Press.

Shengold, L. 1989. *Soul Murder: The Effects of Childhood Abuse and Deprivation*. New Haven: Yale University Press.

Shusterman, R. 1988. "Postmodernist Aestheticism." *Theory, Culture and Society* 5 (June): 350.

Sinha, S. Prakash. 1971. *Asylum and International Law*. The Hague: Martinus Nijhoff.

Smith, R. D., et al. 1982. *Multiple Personality: Theory, Diagnosis, and Treatment*. New York: Irvington.

Sprengnether, M. 1990. *The Spectral Mother: Freud, Feminism, and Psychoanalysis*. Ithaca: Cornell University Press.

Stam, R. 1988. "Mikhail Bakhtin and Left Cultural Critique." In E. Ann Kaplan, ed., *Postmodernism and Its Discontents*. New York: Verso.

Stanton, D. C. 1986. "Difference on Trial: A Critique of the Maternal Metaphor in Cixous, Irigaray, and Kristeva" In N. K. Miller, ed., *The Poetics of Gender.* New York: Columbia University Press, 1986.

Sukenick, R. 1969. "The Death of the Novel." In *The Death of the Novel and Other Stories.* New York: Dial.

Sullivan, H. S. 1952. *Schizophrenia as a Human Process.* New York: Norton.

Szasz, T. S. 1961. *The Myth of Mental Illness.* New York: Delta.

——. 1970. *Ideology and Insanity.* New York: Doubleday.

Turkle, S. 1980. "French Anti-Psychiatry." In D. Ingleby, ed., *Critical Psychiatry.* New York: Pantheon.

Valenstein, A. F. 1989. Pre-oedipal Constructions in Psychoanalysis." *International Journal of Psycho-Analysis*, 70: 433–42.

Volkan, V. 1988. *The Need to Have Enemies and Allies: From Clinical Practice to International Relationships.* Northvale, N.J.: J. Aronson.

Warner, R. 1985. *Recovery from Schizophrenia: Psychiatry and Political Economy.* Boston: Routledge and Kegan Paul.

Weedon, C. 1987. *Feminist Practice and Poststructuralist Theory.* New York: Basil Blackwell.

Wilde, A. 1981. *Horizons of Assent: Modernism, Postmodernism, and the Ironic Imagination.* Baltimore: Johns Hopkins University Press.

Winnicott, D. W. 1953. "Transitional Objects and Transitional Phenomena." *International Journal of Psychoanalysis* 34: 89–97.

——. 1965. *The Maturational Processes and the Facilitating Environment: Studies in the Theory of Emotional Development.* New York: International Universities Press.

——. 1971. "Mirror-Role of Mother and Family in Child Development." In Winnicott, *Playing and Reality*, pp. 111–18. New York: Basic Books.

——. 1982. *Playing and Reality.* New York: Tavistock.

Wittgenstein, L. 1953. *Philosophical Investigations.* Trans. G. E. M. Anscombe. New York: The Macmillan Company.

Wolfenstein, E. V. Forthcoming. *Psychoanalytic Marxism: (Groundwork).* New York: Guilford Press.

INDEX

Library of Congress Cataloging-in-Publication Data

Glass, James M.
   Shattered selves : multiple personality in a postmodern world /
James. M. Glass.
     p. cm.
   Includes bibliographical references and index.
   ISBN 0-8014-2809-2 (alk. paper)
    1. Multiple personality—Political aspects. 2. Postmodernism—
Psychological aspects. 3. Cultural psychiatry. 4. Psychoanalysis and feminism. I. Title.
RC569.5.M8G58   1993
305.9'0824—dc20   92-33928